I WOKE UP WITH MY MIND ON FREEDOM

JANICE KELSEY

Janice Wesley Kelsey

urbanpress

I Woke Up with My Mind on Freedom
by Janice Kelsey

ISBN 978-1-63360-068-3
For Worldwide Distribution

Printed in the U.S.A.

Cover photo courtesy of A. Boswell Photography

Cover photo is part of the *Four Spirits* sculpture in Kelly Ingram Park, erected in 2013 to honor the four girls killed in the 16th Street Baptist Church bombing.

Urban Press
P.O. Box 8881
Pittsburgh, PA 15221-0881
412.646.2780
www.urbanpress.us

DEDICATION

This book is dedicated to memory of my mother, Mrs. Katye Ruth Williams Wesley, whose life of service and sacrifice instilled in me the courage to stand up for what was right. Her guiding principle to each of her children was "In all thy ways acknowledge Him and He shall direct that paths." To my grand-children, Andrew, William, Kayce, Kelsey and Zachary, I leave a legacy to continue the fight for freedom and justice whenever and wherever you find inequities.

In jail with friends and fellow marchers

INTRODUCTION

You may be asking why I would want to write a book about something that happened more than 50 years ago. I was arrested in 1963 while participating in the Children's Crusade in my home town of Birmingham, Alabama. I can still remember the events like they happened yesterday. I suppose someone who is arrested would tend to remember such an event, especially as a kid. While those images of the police, my schoolmates marching with me, and the sights and sounds of that day are etched in my mind, over the years I have read other accounts of the events that surrounded those tumultuous days in 1963, and some of them don't sound quite familiar. Whether embellished or "re-worked" as I like to say, certain accounts just don't quite register with me and I was there. I vividly remember every detail.

Therefore, I've had it in my heart to record my memories so generations to come will have my view of what happened. I also want it to be known how Black people felt before and after the 1963 revolts. I want the generations to come to understand that what I lived through, along with so many others, is not part of ancient history. It's part of modern American history. I also want my family members, grandchildren, and great grandchildren to be able to read and know what part their family played in helping to make a difference in the lives of many others, for that Children's Crusade did indeed change history—and those changes are still being sought 50 years later. I am 69 years old as I start to write, so if I want to leave a written legacy, I had better do it now!

As I write (in 2016), young people who are the age I was in 1963 are leaving their schools to protest a recent presidential election. I admire young people who have the courage to express themselves in a legal way, and I am proud of the fact that they have the right to protest in this country. What they are intending to do today, however, is not the same as our intent in 1963. Even as a young person, I was personally denied rights and privileges that should have been mine as an American citizen. The young people protesting now are upset about what could happen if the presidential election turns out a certain way. That's not the situation we lived in when we were attacked and harassed regularly by the authorities in the deep South in the days of Jim Crow. I respect what those young people are doing, but our situation was life and death, and some people did indeed die along the way as they fought to have this country act according to the truth of the Declaration of Independence—that all men and women, including men and women of color, were and are created equal and should have equal protection under the law of our land.

When I protested, marched, and was arrested, I was not after special rights or privileges for me and my people. All I wanted was what is referred to today as a level playing field. I wasn't after job or school admissions quotas. I just wanted a fair chance to live my life as a woman, a wife, a mother, a teacher, and an American citizen. I didn't want anyone to hire me if I wasn't qualified, but I did not want someone not hiring me if I was qualified, just because I was Black.

What made me even more upset as a teenager is that I didn't know how un-level the field was until someone explained it to me. I grew up in a segregated society and it had always been that way. I wasn't bothered by it, because everyone I knew in my community, church, and school looked just like me. I didn't feel different. I didn't know, in most instances, that the situation was so much better for White citizens. Of course, I experienced some things I did not like when I was growing up, such as riding the bus where I paid the same amount as everyone, but had to stand, even though there may have been seats available. Those seats, however, were reserved for White people.

When I rode the bus with my school teacher aunt, with whom I lived with for a few years, she would place her hands on my shoulders to keep me in my place. She didn't want me moving into an area that was designated as "Whites only." I didn't really like that, but I didn't think too much about it. I didn't think I could do anything about it, for it was part of our life in Birmingham. What's more, it had always been that way, and we had learned to live with it to survive. It's sort of like learning to play with a toy that is broken; after a while, that's just the way it works and you adapt.

When it was brought to my attention that someone else's school was better than mine, however, and that didn't seem fair to me. When someone else had textbooks that were more current and relevant than the ones I had or when I was paying more for the same food that someone else was eating, and I couldn't even sit down to eat it in their restaurant, all that began to bother me. That awareness eventually drove me to pursue a society that would allow me to enjoy what was fair, and I still seek to see people treated fairly, no matter who they are. That morning in 1963, I woke up wanting to be free from all the inequities. I didn't want my aunt holding me down anymore. I wanted the same good textbooks that my White counterparts had. Yes, I admit, I woke up that morning and my mind was on freedom! Hence the title of my book.

So, I am going to tell you the story of my arrest at the age of 16, and then I'll tell you my life story that was so profoundly shaped by the Civil Rights Movement, of which my arrest was a part. I am always pleasantly surprised these days when I am called upon to tell my story in cities across the country. I also now serve on the board of directors of the Birmingham Civil Rights Institute, which is another reason I am writing. I want to contribute the account of my journey to the larger, formal narrative of what happened in my city and country. What happened in Birmingham helped shape the Movement, and I am proud that I played a part. I want to document my small splash in such a huge wave, for every step and every splash have counted.

Later in the book, you will hear from my brother and sister. I asked them to contribute because I wanted their story and perspective of my arrest and the events of 1963 to be heard. I must admit I was surprised when I listened to their account, especially the words from my sister, who told me things as I prepared to write this book that I had never heard from her before. We didn't talk about racial issues much back in 1963; we had learned to suppress what we were thinking and feeling out of fear and from a sense of hopelessness that things would never change.

I am honored to have my family as part of this project, and to have their support, for even though this is my story, it's our story, too—along with my fellow pro-freedom citizens of Birmingham. I hope when you finish that you will feel this is a part of your story, for this struggle and my part in it is not only about me or my people, it is about injustice. As Coretta Scott King said about the inauguration of the Martin Luther King National Holiday, "This is not a Black holiday, it's a people's holiday." My story is not a Black story, but rather a people's story, a story that I am privileged to finally tell after all these years.

Janice Wesley Kelsey

CHAPTER ONE
D-DAY

May 2, 1963 began like any other school day. Mama was cooking breakfast for her brood of nine as I got ready to go, packing my things as normal. With so many in the house, it was always a hustle and bustle in the mornings. As usual, Daddy had left for his early work shift, so Mama was left to oversee the hectic pace of getting all of us out to school. Hence, my mother suspected nothing, not noticing that I had packed some "not-so-normal" supplies. I took a toothbrush, toothpaste, deodorant, a change of underwear, and some socks. D-Day, as we were calling it, had arrived. Oh yes, I also wore my older sister's leather jacket, a jacket you'll hear more about later.

I was 16 years old, and I had never even seen a jail, let alone served time in one. I had been preparing for this day by attending training and informational sessions at local churches for several weeks prior. I had learned of the rights that had been denied me and my people of color, and I was ready to do something about it. I had decided that what was happening just wasn't fair.

My mother had the radio on, and though my preparation may have escaped her, I think she sensed something unusual was going on in Birmingham in the Black community. Before I left, she warned me, "Janice, I'm sending you to school. Don't you go anywhere and get yourself in any trouble. I don't have any money to get you out." To which I responded, "Yes ma'am," which is what she needed and wanted to hear. I had been an obedient and compliant child up to that point in my life, and my mother had no reason to expect or anticipate anything less than that.

I did not lie to my mother when I said, "Yes, ma'am." I was going to school. I just wasn't going to *stay* in school. The plan was to go to school and later in the morning, we planned to walk out and protest in the city streets. As we walked to school, we were singing freedom songs like, *Oh Freedom*, and *We Shall Overcome.* We were taking roll, so to speak, seeing who was walking with us and who was going to participate in D-Day for sure. The people I was walking with were just as excited as I was. We had prepared and were in it together, and D-Day seemed like the right thing to do. I had no fearful thoughts or regrets about my decision. You could say I woke up with my mind on freedom.

We got to school and went to our first period class as normal. When the bell rang, however, we didn't go on to our next class. We marched right for the front door and walked out of school. There were many of us and we walked from my school to 16th Street Baptist Church. That wasn't a real long walk, maybe a couple of miles, and we always walked anywhere we went in those days, so it wasn't a big deal. We were so excited about D-Day that four or five miles did not bother us!

We arrived at the church and there were many people already there. Kids of all sizes and ages from different schools had already created a large gathering. James Bevel (minister and Civil Rights leader) and Andrew Young (minister and Civil Rights strategist) were the two men in charge. They stood at the top of the church steps and ushered those who had come to participate in the march into the church. We went in and sang more freedom songs; this produced the energy we needed to proceed. Then we recited some prayers and at a certain hour, they lined us up in pairs and we walked out of the church singing *We Shall Overcome.*

We stepped out of the church and we marched two-by-two toward City Hall. We didn't get far at all when a police officer stopped us and spoke through a megaphone. The officer told us that we were in violation of a city ordinance and told us we could not parade without a permit. He told us that we could get out of the line and disperse and nothing would happen to us, but if we chose to stay in line, we would go to jail.

What he said did not bother me. Our leaders had prepared us in our training sessions for this. What did bother and intimidate me was his very presence, for I was not accustomed to disobeying adults and had never done so in my young life. What's more, I had never had a confrontation with a White man before. This White man was wearing a gun and had a stick in his hand, and it was an intimidating sight for a girl of sixteen who had never been in any kind of trouble. As the officer waited, someone started singing *We Are Not Afraid* and it resonated throughout the crowd. That song gave me the courage I needed to remain in the line, though my mind had wavered for a second or two.

I don't think anyone left the line, and after a few minutes, we were told we were under arrest. They called for the police vehicles that were going to take us to jail. We were told in our training sessions that we should only give our names and ages and not our addresses or parent's names, because there could be repercussions. If we told them where we lived, the Klan could do something to our homes or our parents could have lost their jobs. Therefore, we only gave our names and ages just as we had been instructed. My girlfriends and I had decided to say we were 15 so all of us would hopefully go to the same place. I had already turned 16, but I said I was 15 so we could stay together.

We were placed in a "paddy wagon", which was like a truck van with bars on the windows, probably built to hold about four prisoners. But they packed us in those wagons, and we sat on top of each other as more and more of our friends were told to get in. That didn't bother us, and we were rocking the van and singing as loudly as we could. When we got to the county jail, it was more structured and orderly, and we were lined up until it was time to give our fingerprints and take our mug shots. Some of the children, were questioned as the police were processing our arrests. I wasn't among those questioned.

All this may sound strange to you, and you may be asking questions like: Why would adults prepare so many youth and children to go to jail? Why didn't the adults go to jail? What could be so wrong that that we were willing to risk so much? Why were we so sure we were doing the right thing?

These are relevant questions and I'm glad you asked. A

part of me being able to answer will rest with my giving you a view into my family life, life in Birmingham for a Black citizen in that day, and other circumstances that led to the Children's Crusade. Let's get started.

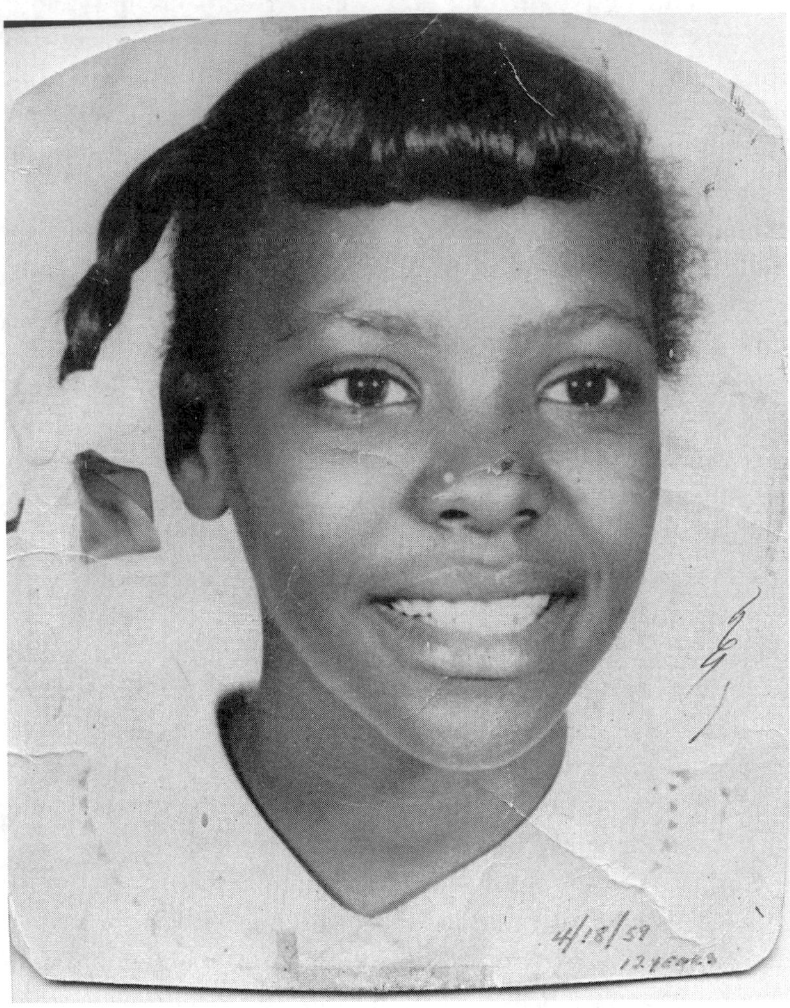

CHAPTER TWO

THE WAY THINGS WERE

I was born in Birmingham on April 18, 1947, number five of a sibling clan that what would eventually turn into nine. I was the second girl. My older brothers and I were close in age and we were a part of a close-knit family. Since we were close to the same age, we encountered almost the same things. Our parents imparted the same values and instilled a common discipline for us all—school, church, respect, and hard work. These were the values we witnessed in our parents, and these were the values they preached to us on a regular basis.

My mother worked sometimes during our growing up years. She sold insurance for a while at Booker T. Washington's Insurance, a Black-owned insurance company, and had other jobs as well. My father worked as a laborer at Tennessee Coal and Iron. I thought we had a pretty normal life. As did most Black families back then, we always went to church on Sundays, and our activities and social lives revolved around what was going on in church, the neighborhood, and school.

What I didn't realize until my awakening in high school was that our world had been shrunk to our church, our Black neighborhoods and our schools due to segregation. We were not permitted to interface freely in White culture, so we had to develop our own and stay there unless specifically invited to come out of it for work or a special occasion. The call for work or one of those special occasions was never a decision that rested with us.

Birmingham was one of the most racially divided cities in the United States, and as I mentioned earlier, segregation was enforced by law, and it was deeply entrenched by tradition. Dr. Martin Luther King, Jr. once stated that Birmingham was the most segregated city in the nation. Everything was segregated: schools, public parks, movie theaters, hotels, churches, and entire communities. Everything was described in terms of "us" and "them". I didn't know much about "them" because I had no reason to go into an area that was designated as "White." As I rode on city buses, I could not sit in seats reserved for Whites. Even if there were seats available in the front, I could not sit in that area. If the bus was crowded, I would pay the fare in the front of the bus, get off and enter the side door of the bus where I was required to stand. There was one theater where Blacks and Whites could attend a movie "together." Blacks would pay at the ticket booth, and then walk around the corner to go up the fire escape to the balcony to watch the movie.

Police officers disrespected adult men, often referring to them as boys and women as girls or gals. No Black adult was addressed as Mister or Misses. White men who worked the same jobs were paid more than their Black counterparts. Police officers would intimidate Black youth and call them to the police car for questioning and sometimes roll the window up on their necks.

White children in schools referred to Black custodians and cafeteria workers by their first names. Rules that came to be known as Jim Crow laws were in effect, which made it illegal for Black children and White children to play a game of ball, checkers, or chess with one another. A Black citizen could not eat in a food establishment unless an eight-foot wall was erected to divide the two races. To prevent integration of the parks and pools as was required by law, Birmingham closed all city parks in the 1960s rather than open them for use by White and Black together.

Civil rights leaders like Rev. Fred Shuttlesworth were beaten and arrested for attempting to enroll Black children in an all-White school. Because Rev. Shuttlesworth was quite vocal about the disrespect shown to people of color, his home and church were bombed on more than one occasion. There were so many unsolved bombings of homes and churches of prominent civil rights activists and Black citizens that eventually Birmingham became known as "Bombingham." The bombings went unsolved because local authorities never investigated to see who planned or carried them out; but everyone knew they were done by members of the Ku Klux Klan, often with police help and protection.

In 1960, 35% of Birmingham's population was Black, yet only 5% of the Black population was registered and permitted to vote in a general election. My people were regularly subjected to special rules and regulations that kept them from voting. Things like poll taxes, literacy tests, and other contrivances existed for the sole purpose of keeping us away from the ballot box.

That segregation carried over into the areas of education where the law of our land was separate but equal. That meant that Black students went to their own schools (separate) but our schools were anything but equal. We had inferior facilities and supplies, although our Black teachers were among the finest instructors in the country. Lucky for us, most all educators in that day were proud of the responsibilities that had been entrusted to them.

I attended Washington Elementary School and Ullman High School. I knew we had great teachers who cared and gave a lot of themselves. Teaching was one profession that people of color had gravitated towards, for many felt education was a key to Black Americans overcoming the terrible injustices and inequities of life in America, especially in the South. When I was growing up, some of our finest and smartest became teachers because it was one way they could serve their people and improve their future conditions. This is what prompted my decision to become a teacher as well.

When I was in the third grade, I went to live with my mother's sister who only lived about three blocks from our house. Aunt Edith had a son who graduated from Ullman High School and had gone on to Fisk University in Nashville. Since she was alone, I moved in with her and went to school where she taught at W. C. Davis Elementary. It started out with me spending the night sometimes and eventually my aunt asked my parents to allow me to stay with her to give her some company in her home. This arrangement afforded me extra privileges I may not have had living with my parents and siblings. I was chosen to go and live with her because I was a girl, and my sister was six years older than I and already in high school. My brothers weren't an option. I think my father wanted to keep a closer watch on them.

Living with her created a good life for me; it was like being the only child. My aunt would buy my clothes and take me on vacation with her. All the while, I had the fun and comfort of a big family only three short blocks away. I would see them almost every day, and especially on weekends.

The Black family was the main unit of the Black community and our family was no different. Church was the focus of that life, and school was important. I never thought much of what we had or didn't have. I just knew we were together and loved one another. It was the same for all my friends, and that was the way I thought it was always going to be. In fact, I didn't realize that we were considered "poor" until I took a sociology class in college and found that our family income would put us in that classification.

I was always an honor roll student. I was often awarded for having a perfect attendance record. When I entered the eighth grade, I transferred from Davis school where my aunt taught, to Washington School in our neighborhood. Since all my siblings had graduated from eighth grade there, I wanted to follow suit. Washington School was only one block away from our house and four blocks from Aunt Edith's.

After I transferred to Washington School, I remember a teacher telling me I had the highest score on the California Achievement Test of anyone in the school. This gave me great confidence in my academic abilities and I continued to be a good student. I graduated from Ullman High School, ranking in the top ten of my class. When I graduated from Miles College, I was in the top ten of my graduating class. I have always done well academically and I attribute that in part to the dedicated Black teachers who served in our schools. They were on a mission to improve the conditions of their people.

As I stated, our lives revolved around the church. I sang in the choir, the Sunbeam Band, and the Red Circles. We attended everything that went on in church: Sunday school, youth meetings, Easter plays, Christmas programs, and picnics. My father was a deacon, my mother taught Sunday school, and she was also the Vacation Bible School director. The church was three blocks from where we lived. As I told you, our lives seldom moved out of the circle of our neighborhood. I wasn't aware of the restraints of that circle until I got a little older and learned about the hostile world that existed almost across the street from where I was raised.

In high school, I often participated in school plays. I was a member of the Drama Club, The Thespians, and a social club called Las Amigas. My life was centered around being outgoing and popular and I was basically enjoying life. I never had a chance to encounter people of a different race or religion. I thought all was well with the world, at least the one I lived in. When I read the newspapers, I was not particularly interested in what was being reported. I chose to read the *Dear Abby* column and the comics section. My leisure reading focused on romance novels and other normal interests for a teen girl.

All that began to change, however, because I had a girlfriend whose mother and sister were involved in what we called "the Movement," which of course was the Civil Rights Movement. Grenetta would come to school and talk about what happened at the mass meetings. What she said caught my attention. Her sister and her mother were in the mass movement's choir, and she boasted about how great the music was. She also related how well all the ministers at the meetings could speak—and how well they dressed. She talked about all the cute boys who attended those meetings. It seemed to me that everybody who was "somebody" was going to the mass meetings, and that's why I felt the need to go.

Now, let me tell you a bit about why these mass meetings were being held and why the Movement, which I will call the Civil Rights Movement from this point forward, came to be so important to Birmingham.

CHAPTER THREE

MY WAKE-UP CALL

The mass meetings were held at different churches across the city. The first one I went to was held at New Pilgrim Baptist Church. It was within walking distance of our home, and my mother allowed my brother and me to walk together to the meeting. When I arrived, it was everything my girlfriend had described and more. It was so exciting! I could not believe how large the crowds were and the music certainly impressed me. The choir, under the direction of a man named Carlton Reese, was just outstanding. As music director for the ACMHR (Alabama Christian Movement for Human Rights), Reese adapted many traditional hymns into what we referred to as "freedom songs" for the choir, which performed at all the evening mass meetings. He could make sounds on that organ like I had never heard before. I was in awe.

It was also exciting for me to see the people from various churches across the city who made up the choir. They wore different colored robes that were monogrammed, and it was a beautiful sight just to look at them. It seemed to me that everyone in the choir knew how to sing. I had to laugh because at my home church, it seemed that people didn't really have to know how to sing to be in the choir, but this choir was impressive. As good as the sights and sounds of the meeting were, what got me involved in the movement was what happened after all the pageantry was finished. After the preliminaries, Rev. James Bevel called the teenagers to meet with him in the church's annex.

All of the ministers on the platform, and there were many, were dressed well in three-piece suits and they spoke eloquently. I don't remember what they said, but they sounded great. People enthusiastically responded to what they were saying. When Rev. Bevel came on stage, he was not dressed like any of them. He had on denim overalls, and wore a little beanie cap on the back of his head. He had a light-skinned complexion, and we thought light-skinned equated to being good looking. He impressed me when I saw him come forward looking so different than the rest of the ministers.

Rev. Bevel was young, like us, and invited all of us to move away from where the adults were to another area. I was eager to hear what he had to say, and what he had to say for me was an eye-opening education. Rev. Bevel educated us through a series of questions concerning the inequities of life that we had grown accustomed to in Birmingham. The more I learned, the more I wanted to be involved. The more I listened, the more my mind became impregnated with the prospect of doing something to address those wrongs. It just wasn't fair, or so it seemed to me and many others.

I eventually learned that Rev. Bevel was the mastermind behind the Children's Crusade strategy. He was one of the leaders in the Southern Christian Leadership Conference (SCLC), the organization headed by Dr. Martin Luther King, Jr. Bevel had convinced Dr. King to allow students to participate in protest marches in Birmingham, Alabama, since the Civil Rights Movement had encountered such a difficult time gaining any momentum in my city. The fear and intimidation of my people was such that few wanted to risk their livelihoods, families, and lives to stand up to the establishment and oppose the lack of justice for Blacks. Rev. Bevel thought that children protesting would direct the country's attention to the problems of segregation.

It was probably April of 1963 when we gathered, and the first thing Rev. Bevel did was poll the audience, asking what schools we attended. When he called out a school's name, we cheered, and it sounded like a school pep rally. Once he determined who was present and settled us down, he started asking us questions. For example, he asked if anyone at Ullman High School took a typing class. I raised my hand, because I was a good typist and didn't mind letting him know.

He then asked me how many electric typewriters I had in my school. I answered that we had one and I got to type on it because I was a good typist. He said, "You have one? Do you know how many they have at Phillips High School?" Phillips was an all-White school, and of course, I didn't know the answer since I had never been there. Rev. Bevel informed us that Phillips had three rooms, not three typewriters, but three rooms filled with electric typewriters. He said they didn't even practice on the manual typewriters like we had at our school. When I heard that, I thought, *That's not fair.*

Then he asked if any of the boys played football at Ullman where my brother played. Rev. Bevel asked if we knew why the helmets were always blue and white when we got them, while the school colors were green and grey? My brother responded that they always painted them the right colors, and he had never given that any thought. Rev. Bevel informed us that we were receiving Ramsay High School's discards, and Ramsay was an all-White school about five or six blocks from our school. By now, you know what I thought; *That's not fair either.*

He continued with questions, not just about Ullman, but about a lot of other life issues. He asked if we had every paid attention to the copyright dates in our books. I never had, but he advised us to look at the next chance we had. Sure enough, the books we were using were outdated and had been passed to us after White schools were finished with them because they received new ones.

Then he asked a question that hit me in the very core of my being. He asked if any of us had eaten downtown at one of what we called the "five-and-dime" stores called J.J. Newbury's. They had a beautiful lunch counter on the first floor with leather seats, but of course people of color could not sit in that area. I knew we had to go up to the fourth floor where there was a lunch counter in the back where we could get a hot dog and a Coke for 27 cents. He asked us how much the people who sat in their leather seats paid for the same order, and I thought to myself that it was probably a dollar. Nope. Rev. Bevel enlightened us that they paid the same 27 cents. They paid the same and yet we stood to eat while they sat in the nice seats at the counter.

By the time he finished with his line of questioning, I was convinced I had been thoroughly mistreated. In my mind and heart I said, "Yeah, I'm in this." He told us if we wanted to do something about this, we could. Our parents couldn't, because if they got involved they would go to jail and lose their jobs. If they went to jail, there would be no one to take care of us. They had a lot to lose, he told us. But by comparison, what did we have to lose? We were getting a second-class education, so we had that to lose, but it was worth protesting to try and get a first-class education. I agreed with Rev. Bevel, and that's what got me involved. I thought, "If I can do something about this situation, that is what I want to do."

The follow up to those mass meetings was training sessions where we would be introduced to the concept of non-violent protesting. These sessions were held at churches like 16th Street Baptist (in the basement) or at Saint Paul's, the church right down the street from 16th Street Baptist. Some meetings were at A.G. Gaston Motel, the black-owned motel in the city where Blacks were welcomed. I don't recall how we found out where the meetings would be held, but we did because everyone in my world was talking about it.

At the meetings I attended, we would sing freedom songs to encourage and inspire us. Lyrics of one song included:

Ain't gonna let nobody turn me around
Turn me around, turn me around
Ain't gonna let nobody turn me around
I'm gonna keep on a-walkin', keep on a-talkin'
Marchin' up to freedom land

They showed us films of people who had demonstrated in other cities, and we saw how they had been spit on and struck. The message was that we could not react or respond to any kind of bad treatment we might encounter. The protest was a nonviolent movement, so if we couldn't handle that, they didn't want us marching. They warned that we were going to be called ugly names and might even be hit and injured. We were trained to respond by singing a freedom song, bowing on our knees, covering our head for protection, and saying a prayer. If we couldn't handle that, they told us not to sign up to do anything public. Instead, we would be given something else to do to help the Movement. There were behind-the-scenes tasks, things like making posters or helping the organizers with other clerical duties. If we wanted to march, we had to commit to be nonviolent. I made the commitment.

My determination was to do whatever it took to make a difference. I thought if they (White folks) saw that I could behave and control myself, then we could earn a level playing field where we would be treated fairly in school and at work. My hope was that life would improve and we would be treated more fairly if my friends and I could prove that we were willing to stand up for what was right. I hoped our protest would earn us respect, but it would be years before that would occur. I found out there were some people who would never respect us, no matter how nobly we behaved or how just our cause. That was the nature of the prejudice and hatred that plagued Birmingham and the South that we knew.

My brother was on the football team and his heart, soul, and body were into playing. He has said on several occasions that if he had walked out with us on D-Day, he would have missed football practice. If he missed practice, he would sit on the bench and not play in the game. True to his word, he did not miss football practice on D-Day. Two or three days later, however, he was downtown and was arrested, too. You will hear more about his story as we go on.

I don't remember how many training sessions we attended. A lot of the information was passed by word of mouth, and radio disc jockeys also played an important part in spreading the word and communicating to us. The disc jockey would say certain phrases or play specific songs that were indicators to us that something was happening or about to happen. Because I was with the in-crowd, I knew what was going on and was on the same page as everyone else.

I didn't talk to my parents about what I was doing,

thinking, or feeling. They didn't ask, but certainly my mother was aware that there were rumblings and rumors about what we were going to do. There was not a family discussion about it or warnings about what not to do. It wasn't really until D-Day that she warned me and told me to go to school and stay out of trouble.

We were not a family of civil rights activists, but I did learn something about my mother that made me think that perhaps she would have done what I did if she had the chance. On September 10, 1957, my mother was working as a salad maker in the cafeteria at Woodlawn High School, which was an all-White school. On that day, three effigies of Black figures with racial slurs were raised at Woodlawn, and the Confederate flag was run up the flagpole, according to *The Birmingham News*. When she saw this, she took her apron off and walked home. She was incensed by that behavior, which didn't even seem to be addressed or corrected by school officials. For her to walk home was quite a walk, probably more than ten miles. I would like to think I was following in my mother's footsteps as I decided to walk in the Crusade. Many years later, poetic justice would place my younger brother, Michael, in position as the first Black principal of Woodlawn.

Our leaders warned us that if we got out and participated, we would be arrested. We were told to take some personal items to school with us, like toothpaste, soap, and a change of underwear, because we were going to jail. They told us it may be cold in the jail, so we'd better take a sweater or a jacket with us. All my friends and I were excited, confirming with each other to ensure that everyone was still "in." We double checked to make sure everyone had their supplies. We planned everything in secret. The excitement was intense.

I had one girlfriend whose parents worked for a White family where her father was a chauffeur and her mother was a housekeeper. Her parents told her that she couldn't get involved in anything because if she was caught, they wouldn't be able to "work for those folks anymore." Although she was aware and sympathetic, she couldn't participate. I understood that and I wasn't offended by her absence. My father worked for TC&I with hundreds of other Black men, and I figured they weren't going to single him or any of the other fathers out if we marched. I was never worried that my actions would bring repercussions to my family.

We sang more songs with lyrics that spoke to the heart of what we were going to do:

We're marching on to freedom land.
We're marching on to freedom land.
Thus our strength from day to day
As we walk the narrow way
We're going forward, we're going forward
One day we're going to be free.

There was a song out by Sam Cooke at the time called, *A Change is Gonna Come.* The djs would play that tune, and the message would resonate, particularly with me. When I heard it, I would think, "Oh yeah, I'm anticipating this change that was going to come." We were ready to go and just waiting for the day to arrive.

CHAPTER FOUR

THE BIGGER PICTURE

At this point, you may think it unusual that I was so surprised at the unequal treatment my people were receiving in Birmingham and in American culture in general, especially in the South. You may also be wondering how things got to be the way they were, so let me stop, go back, and explain why there was even a need to protest at all in 1963. I have told you some of the background, but now let me give you more detail. Of course, I will have to reach back long before I was born to trace the history of segregation in the South, and will only provide a cursory overview.

After the Civil War, the South was in shambles as America tried to rebuild and reconcile the massive differences between Black and White. Expectations were high among freed slaves that they were finally going to be part of American life as equals with whites, but those same whites who had lost the War were not about to give up their privileged position. Over time, they sought successfully to reinstitute their supremacy over the Black population through intimidation and by carefully controlling who had the right to vote.

When Blacks were given the right to vote by the Fourteenth Amendment of the Constitution, passed in 1868, there was a provision that allowed state assemblies to regulate voting procedures. After the Amendment, Blacks began to win elected offices in some Southern states, much to the chagrin of their White counterparts. Therefore, the white populace began passing laws that required citizens to be able to read, write, or own property before they could vote. This was all specifically geared toward taking the vote away from Black citizens and it was successful.

When the Federal government pulled its troops out of the South in 1877, who were there in part to protect the rights of

Black citizens, violence against Blacks increased dramatically. All that was part of the plan to intimidate and control Black voters and citizens, and there was not much to stop that from happening. Lynching of Blacks became an issue by the beginning of the 20th century, and in 1915, the Ku Klux Klan became the official force to reckon with in the South; their counterparts had been acting well before that.

Due to the dangers as well as through enforced discrimination in housing, lack of police protection, and separate-but-equal school laws (Black schools were separate but were anything but equal to White schools, with fewer resources and less funding), Blacks increasingly had to live together in areas of any city where they could shield and protect themselves from white domination. What's more, Blacks did not have access to economic opportunities, so poverty was a way of life for most Black citizens, thus causing them to live in substandard housing and attend substandard schools.

Birmingham was not exempt from all these problems that I have described. In fact, for some reason, Birmingham seemed to take segregation and hatred to a new level. While that was happening, the burgeoning iron ore and steel industries provided low-paying jobs for unskilled Black laborers, so the Black population grew in Birmingham, which only caused fearful whites to find new ways to control blacks through legislation and intimidation.

Besides the Klan's actions, the Black citizens were controlled through a series of laws that came to be known as Jim Crow laws. These were laws that segregated drinking fountains, pubic facilities, schools, public transportation, and almost any other aspect of public life. Jim Crow laws were the reason water fountains had signs above them read "Colored Only," and it was against the law for a person of color to drink from a "Whites Only" fountain.

For obvious reasons, Black citizens were careful and cautious about where they went, what they did, and who they trusted. We stayed to ourselves in our churches, schools, and

civic organizations. When I was born, that was how it w
didn't know anything else. I never saw White folks, except
I went downtown and saw them shopping and eating at places where I could not go.

I may be wrong, but it seems like the Klan and the government in both my state and city took segregation and violence to unprecedented levels. That is why Dr. Martin Luther King, Jr. and other civil rights leaders began to focus their efforts on Birmingham to try and bring social justice in the early 1960s. At that time, our governor was a man by the name of George C. Wallace. He was first elected in 1962 and quickly became the face of White supremacy in the South and the nation. During his inauguration speech, Governor Wallace uttered the famous phrase, "segregation now, segregation tomorrow, segregation forever," and that had basically been his message during the campaign. In June 1963, Governor Wallace stood in the door of the University of Alabama to block the registration of the first Black student.

In 1962, students from Miles College (my alma mater) led a selective buying campaign. At that time, it was illegal in the state of Alabama to organize a boycott against a business or service. Therefore, the decision was made to ask parents to refrain from buying Easter clothes for their children. A few students stood outside large department stores in downtown Birmingham trying to discourage Black shoppers from making purchases in stores where they weren't allowed to sit and eat lunch. Many pastors joined in the effort by encouraging the children to wear their old clothes or jeans for Easter. Because of this campaign, the downtown stores saw a 48% decline in their sales that spring. This effort was the precursor to what took place the next year.

In April of 1963, one month before I was arrested, Dr. King along with the Southern Christian Leadership Conference (SCLC) decided to target Birmingham during the Easter season by pressuring merchants to hire more black employees. Dr. King joined forces with Birmingham's pastor and founder of the Alabama Christian Movement for Human Rights (ACMHR), Rev. Fred Shuttlesworth. On April 3, 1963, Dr. King, SCLC, and ACMHR began their protests against segregation with a series of mass meetings, lunch counter sit-ins, and other nonviolent means of protest. Eugene "Bull" Connor, who was our commissioner of public safety and a renowned racist, began to arrest protesters and even Dr. King was arrested on Good Friday when he ignored a court order that banned protests. While Dr. King was confined in solitary confinement, he wrote his famous *Letter from the Birmingham Jail* in response to criticism from white clergymen about his role in the protests.

When I read that letter, I am still moved by its passion and eloquence, especially since Dr. King wrote it in prison without proper writing paper or utensils. I urge you to read the Letter in its entirety, but let me include some of what Dr. King wrote to help you understand the climate in Birmingham as we marched and went to jail:

> *I think I should indicate why I am here in Birmingham, since you have been influenced by the view which argues against "outsiders coming in." I have the honor of serving as president of the Southern Christian Leadership Conference, an organization operating in every southern state, with headquarters in Atlanta, Georgia. We have some eighty-five affiliated organizations across the South, and one of them is the Alabama Christian Movement for Human Rights. Frequently we share staff, educational and financial resources with our affiliates. Several months ago, the affiliate here in Birmingham asked us to be on call to engage in a nonviolent direct action program if such were deemed necessary. We readily consented, and when the hour came we lived up to our promise. So I, along with several members of my staff, am here because I was invited here. I am here because I have organizational ties here.*
>
> *But more basically, I am in Birmingham because injustice is here. Just as the prophets of the eighth century B.C.*

left their villages and carried their "thus saith the Lord" far beyond the boundaries of their home towns, and just as the Apostle Paul left his village of Tarsus and carried the gospel of Jesus Christ to the far corners of the Greco Roman world, so am I compelled to carry the gospel of freedom beyond my own home town. Like Paul, I must constantly respond to the Macedonian call for aid.

Moreover, I am cognizant of the interrelatedness of all communities and states. I cannot sit idly by in Atlanta and not be concerned about what happens in Birmingham. Injustice anywhere is a threat to justice everywhere. We are caught in an inescapable network of mutuality, tied in a single garment of destiny. Whatever affects one directly, affects all indirectly. Never again can we afford to live with the narrow, provincial "outside agitator" idea. Anyone who lives inside the United States can never be considered an outsider anywhere within its bounds.

You deplore the demonstrations taking place in Birmingham. But your statement, I am sorry to say, fails to express a similar concern for the conditions that brought about the demonstrations. I am sure that none of you would want to rest content with the superficial kind of social analysis that deals merely with effects and does not grapple with underlying causes. It is unfortunate that demonstrations are taking place in Birmingham, but it is even more unfortunate that the city's white power structure left the Negro community with no alternative.

(Copied from: https://www.africa.upenn.edu/Articles_Gen/Letter_Birmingham.html)

With many adults scared to participate in the protests, it was then that Rev. James Bevel proposed using children to increase the momentum. That is what became known as the Children's Crusade, of which I was a part. Thus, the attention of our nation was on Birmingham during those fateful days in April and May of 1963.

Against this historical backdrop, I and my fellow students

answered Rev. Bevel's call to march in Birmingham so that we could continue the work of Dr. King, Rev. Shuttlesworth, and so many other dedicated leaders. There was criticism for sure that they were calling on youth to continue the dangerous work, but we were finally aware and awakened to what was going on, and we were ready to march. Let's go back now and pick up the story of what happened on May 2 and the days following during the 1963 Birmingham civil rights protests.

CHAPTER FIVE

D-DAY COMES TO LIFE

As I considered my involvement in what came to be known as the Children's Crusade, I did have some personal concerns about the possible ramifications of my stand. I had a good grade point average and really didn't want to mess that up in any way. Therefore, I spoke to my young first period teacher who I thought was approachable. I asked her hypothetically, "if some kids walked out of class, are they going to fail?" and she said, "If everyone walks, there's no one to fail." That answer gave me the certainty that the school officials were not going to do anything to us if we participated in the march. That teacher gave me a pass to go, and that lessened my anxiety about what was going to happen to me. Of course, I shared that information with everyone I talked to, informing them that the administrators weren't going to do anything to us. That was the first thing I wanted to clear up.

We were told when the bell sounded for classes to change that it was time to go. There were people running down the halls yelling, "It's time! It's time!" Right then, folks started walking out. One teacher, who later spoke about the march, said that she simply turned her back and started writing on the board. She said the teachers could not tell us it was okay to go, but they couldn't do anything to really stop us from leaving, especially if they didn't notice us leaving. As I look back, it is my opinion that if the teachers had stood fast and said we had better not do this, I might not have gone. I had a tremendous amount of respect for teachers, and I thought their authority was an important thing. I would not have disrespected a teacher. Since they didn't do anything to cause me to think that I was going to regret my actions, I felt better about leaving.

I didn't think much ahead about what we would encounter when we marched downtown. That Commissioner of

Public Safety, Eugene "Bull" Connor, had gained national and international attention for his cruelty and violence used to enforce segregation. I had never seen Bull Connor in action, but I knew his name and knew he was a powerful man. I didn't know enough about him to be afraid of what he might do. I wasn't even aware that the citizens of Birmingham had tried to vote him out of office, and he was in the midst of a court proceeding to protest that effort. I didn't realize that because I wasn't reading the local newspaper, but it has been alleged that a lot of the reporting in the *Birmingham News* at that time was less than accurate.

There were things that maybe I should have known, that I did not know. I did not hear my parents discussing anything about the conditions and situation in Birmingham. When they were engaged in conversations, they put us out of the room. We were not permitted to sit around while adults talked, so I didn't get a lot of negative information. Of course, our parents were trying to protect us and to keep us safe, for living in a segregated city meant that we pretty much had to keep to ourselves and learn to make do with the businesses and services that were available in our Black communities. We had covered some things in our mass meetings about being prepared and how to protect ourselves, but I am not sure we were ready for the police and firemen responses that included dogs and fire hoses that thrust young protesters down city streets like the tumbleweed seen in cowboy movies.

There were many people in jail with me, many of whom I knew from school and church. I learned later that 973 young people were arrested on D-Day and almost 2,000 were arrested before the marches ceased. I was excited then and today I am still honored to have been part of the group. After we were arrested and had our ride in the paddy wagon, many were taken to what we called Family Court. At that time, Family Court looked to me to be a big house. We were standing around in the front area, shoulder to shoulder, because more and more people kept coming. After a while, there were so many people in there the city officials called for school buses to come and get us. As they lined us up to get on the school buses, we started cheering at the sight of the yellow school buses, which I am sure confused the officials.

We were so excited because Birmingham did not provide yellow school buses for Black students at that time. Therefore, when the yellow school buses pulled up, we cheered and shouted that we were finally going to be allowed on a school bus. We were getting ready to ride what we called the Big Cheese. We got on the Big Cheese and I sat down on the front seat. We started singing freedom songs again and had the greatest time. The yellow school buses carried us from Family Court to the County Courthouse, which was downtown. We got off the buses and walked down a ramp into what looked like a loading dock. They took our possessions (most of which were returned later) as we gave them our names and ages. Fingerprinting continued and they took mugshots.

Then they sent us upstairs to a large area that I would call a day room, which had several individual jail cells. We could walk in between those cells and there was a big door at the end of that corridor. We couldn't get out, but we could move around in there. They had a wooden table in one of them and I think it was a bench, but we chose to sit on each other or on the concrete floor. We slept on the floor our first night in jail. When they served us supper, we were fed by inmates who were called trustees. They were in white uniforms and all of them were asking us as we went through the line why we were there and where we had all come from. We proudly said that we came to get our freedom, and it was an honor to tell them that. Those trustees were all Black men, and I would like to think they were proud of us.

I can't remember why exactly, but I didn't like the food. When we talked among ourselves, the consensus was that it was nasty. I realized I was in jail, but it didn't dawn on me that what I had done might have lifelong consequences. I felt strongly that I was doing the right thing because we had been mistreated and this was the way to correct it.

As others came in, we'd ask each other what school they

were from and what was going on outside with the protests. We still had a sense of excitement and anticipation. We sat around, talked girl talk, and sang more freedom songs. We sat on each other and complained about how cold it was, because they had taken our jackets, purses, and personal belongings so we didn't have anything to help keep us warm. The next day, which was a Friday, the school buses came back and again we cheered as we got out of jail, with no idea about what was next.

More youth arrived and some came in talking about how the police had dogs and water hoses out and how kids were being knocked down by the water. When I got out of jail, I heard from others who talked about being knocked down or pinned against a wall by the water pressure. I had one girlfriend who said some of her hair was sheared off her head by the force of the water. People had blouses torn and reported that their skin was bruised and cut from the force of the water. They talked about trying to get away from the police and all the mayhem. My oldest brother, who was in college at the time, was in Kelly Ingram Park during the protests and reported seeing folks carrying kids with dog bites to the hospital. People were talking for weeks after about the protests, still horrified by the response.

After the county jail, our next stop was a makeshift jail located at the Alabama State Fairgrounds. We used to call that place Kiddieland Park. There was an amusement park there that Blacks weren't allowed to go to, except on Saturday night after 10:00 PM. That's why I had never been there, but had passed it many times when my dad would take us for a ride on Sundays. You could see the lights on the ferris wheel and could almost smell the popcorn and cotton candy. It just looked like a great place to be, but we couldn't go in so we would just drive past and look. I always had a desire to go to Kiddieland Park. Ironically, I got my chance.

When the bus turned into Kiddieland, we went crazy and were screaming, "Oh my gosh, we are going to Kiddieland Park!" Well, they didn't stop at the ferris wheel. They drove around to the back of the fairgrounds and I was assigned to a 4-H (a national youth organization) dormitory. It was a brick building with tile floors, toilets with petitions around them, lockers, and beds. There were face bowls so we could wash our hands and face. Some of the beds had mattresses and others had both a mattress and a sheet. It was a nice building, and I was much happier to be there than on the jailhouse floor.

After my release, I read that 600 young ladies had been housed there. My parents went to church that Sunday, May 5 and all the parents had apparently been encouraged by the minister to go and retrieve their kids. There were rumors circulating about what was happening with the children. Some people were saying the kids were in the same location as the real inmates. That was not the case where I was. I saw the trustees when it was time to serve food, but there was no other interaction with the prisoners. Some students, it was reported, had been released after dark without any notification to parents and were not given a chance to call home. My situation was simply different. My parents came and got me out. I didn't want to go, but I went because I was not in the position to argue with them after having marched without giving them notice or saying what I was going to do. It was time to be submissive.

My parents were not intimidated or harassed in any way about my role in the Crusade. I think all our parents were concerned about what could happen because our protest as well as what could happen to us because of the violent nature of life in a segregated South—especially Birmingham. My father worked at a steel plant and at the time, my mother was working as a practical nurse for a White doctor. I don't think she discussed my involvement in the protest with her employer, but she didn't feel threatened in any way by what happened.

Remember my sister's leather jacket? That was the one instant repercussion that hit my family. Upon my release, the jacket wasn't returned to me. It mysteriously disappeared. With its disappearance came many years of chiding about it from its owner, my sister Elvia. She will have her say about it a bit later.

The makeshift jail at Fair Park

CHAPTER SIX

ARREST AFTERMATH

I was released on Sunday, but could not go back to school on Monday because students who had participated in the demonstrations had been expelled, or at least suspended. Most of my friends were still in jail at that point, so there was no one to talk to or hang out with. My parents' punishment was that I could not use the phone, so I was grounded until things settled down. A news reporter had come in to interview the students when we were housed in the makeshift jail at the fairgrounds. He asked me how I felt about being in jail. At that time, there was a commercial on television for Carnation Milk and the commercial said that Carnation cows were contented. So that's how I responded to his question. I said I was as contented as a Carnation cow! That's when he took the picture that ended up in several national news publications.

I don't remember my parents scolding me when I was released. They did question me about what happened—who I saw, what had been said or done to me. They were more concerned than in the mood to punish me. My brother told me later that the reason he went to jail was because he saw all my mother's anguish about my being in jail. He said she was going on about "Oh Lord, my baby is in jail and I don't know what I am going to do with my baby in jail." He said the worry on her face prompted him to go out and try and get arrested so he could find out what was going on with me. I knew that whatever my parents said or did was out of concern more than out of anger for what I had done.

About a week after the demonstrations began, they subsided. By that following Thursday or Friday, President Kennedy had sent someone to act as a mediator between the SCLC (the Southern Christian Leadership Conference) and city officials to try and bring the Crusade to a close. The leaders of the movement stopped the demonstrations on May 10 when the city officials and merchants downtown agreed to hire at least one Black sales clerk and further agreed to remove signs that read, "Colored Only," which hung above water fountains and restrooms.

While that represented real progress, the A. G. Gaston Motel was bombed on the same day. Dr. King often stayed at that motel when he was in Birmingham, and many of the strategy sessions were held there. In fact, we also had impromptu youth meetings on the lawn of the A.G. Gaston Motel. We soon realized that some people were not going to change and they did not want conditions to change for the better where my people were concerned.

The Birmingham Board of Education was not open to us returning to school. They announced that all students who had participated in the student marches would either be suspended or expelled. One of our local ministers, Rev. Calvin Woods, had daughters who had been arrested. Backed by the NAACP (National Association for the Advancement of Colored People) and then the SCLC, Rev. Woods went to court seeking to overturn the Board's decision to expel us. A local judge ruled in favor of the Board, so Rev. Woods went to Atlanta before the Fifth Circuit Court of Appeals. The lower court's ruling was overturned and the board was admonished for their vindictive action.

The last few weeks of school before summer break were more of a cooling off period than a time for academics. All the demonstrating students were to be reinstated without penalty, and the court ordered that our records be expunged. We were all reinstated before the school year was out, but the fact that I had been arrested remained on my record in defiance of the court's ruling. To the best of my knowledge, however, no one missed graduation because they demonstrated. There were some other consequences, one being the Board's decision to cancel the prom for Black students.

I don't remember having any discussions with adults about what happened. Fear imposed a silence and no one expressed public support for us or for the cause we represented. Of course, some students talked about what we did, who we saw, or what happened to each of us. I don't remember any unusual things other than my brother telling the story of being in jail with the comedian Dick Gregory, who was arrested on May 6, shortly after he arrived in Birmingham and joined the marches.

My involvement and arrest heightened my awareness and desire to know more of what was going on in Birmingham and the nation. As I read the papers and watched the news, I felt a sense of progress and victory for a while. Our President, John F. Kennedy, had intervened and sent someone to Birmingham to help bring things to a close. He also went on national television to talk about what had happened to the children during the demonstrations, calling civil rights a "moral issue." He spoke up quite eloquently on our behalf. I thought a great thing had occurred; I assumed we had overcome.

To see Black sales clerks in downtown businesses was new. We could go into a store and there weren't signs over water fountains; that was new. I thought things were really shaping up. In the fall of 1963, when school opened, my friend Patricia enrolled in West End High School, which was an all-White school. I knew that was an accomplishment and represented real progress. Patricia and I talked on the phone at night and she told me how she was treated (not always well), but she was smart and no one could take that away from her. I didn't recognize the danger that still lurked. I was naïve to think that everyone was happy (or at least tolerant) about what was taking place in the city.

There were fewer mass meetings over the summer break. Some protest activities took place in Florida and I knew some girls who went there with Rev. Bevel to participate. They were arrested there also. I had some friends who rode the buses to the March on Washington in August of 1963, during which Dr. King made his "I Have a Dream" speech. I did not participate in either event, so I had a calm summer. My thought was that those youth probably had parents involved in the protests, so they got included. That was not the case with my family, so I played it cool during an otherwise hot summer.

I was amazed to see the reports and pictures of what did happen and the number of buses and people who went to the March on Washington. I didn't know much of what was going on in Washington other than Dr. King's involvement, but I interpreted everything to indicate that we had overcome, that things were going to keep getting better and better for us. I was elated that I had played some part in this, and had no regrets at all about my role. I had helped make things become fairer, hadn't I?

I was in the second semester of my junior year in the fall (back then we had winter and spring graduations), and it started normally with not much talk about civil rights, other than my friend who was going to West End High School. She reported to me how mean some of the students were to her, calling her names. The teachers ostracized her and wouldn't call on her to answer questions. She was seemingly handling it all well, so I wasn't too concerned. There were mobs and crowds behaving badly and protesting the progress we were making. Maybe I didn't want to see that or maybe it wasn't reported in the news that I was reading and watching. Regardless, the pot was brewing, and in the fall of 1963, something was going to happen in Birmingham, something terrible, that would change my life and the life of our nation in a profound way. Let's turn our attention to that now.

CHAPTER SEVEN

THE UNSPEAKABLE

September 15, 1963 began as any normal Sunday in our house. My mother was cooking breakfast and the aroma filled the house. Kids were scrambling to the bathroom, trying to be the first to get into the tub. We were at the kitchen table where everyone was reciting their Bible verses to prepare for Sunday school while they were eating. That was our normal Sunday routine, and then it was off to church for a good part of the day. My church, South Elyton Baptist Church, was located about three blocks from where I lived. I was off to Sunday school where we were having a special program of some kind. I can't remember what it was, but we had guest teachers coming. When Sunday school was over, a guest presenter was to give us a lesson review.

Mrs. Carter, the guest speaker, was going on and on when our pastor, Rev. Moreland Lanier, who was sitting on a side pew, became a little restless. I attributed his agitation to her being long winded. He finally stood to his feet and interrupted her, apologizing because he had an announcement to make. He said he had terrible news, and had been notified that a bomb had gone off at 16th Street Baptist Church. The exact time of the bombing was 10:22 AM. Naturally, people were shocked and taken aback by the announcement. He said he didn't know what was going on, but he understood there were some casualties, and so he was dismissed church. We were told to go home and pray. Everyone hustled to get home. The assumption, perhaps, was that church was suddenly not a safe place to be.

We got to my house and it didn't take long for our phone to start ringing. People were calling and offering condolences to my parents, saying they heard one of the Wesley girls had been killed. I could hear my parents say that it wasn't our family and no, that it wasn't our child. It started to really impact me on the inside, thinking that someone was calling and asking if

I was dead. I was an energetic teenager. Death wasn't a part of my agenda. I marched. I protested for change. That's what I did. What in the world were these people thinking?

I didn't know anyone in my age group who had ever died. What's more, we weren't talking about a car accident. This happened at church. Bad things weren't supposed to happen at church. Eventually, we got news of the casualties. The first name released was **Cynthia Wesley**, and our family name was Wesley, but Cynthia Wesley and I were not related. She had been adopted and was brought into the home of Claude and Gertrude Wesley. Thus, she assumed their last name.

Mrs. Gertrude Wesley taught school with my aunt Edith Patton, with whom I had lived. When the Wesley's brought Cynthia into their home, I was often invited over for lawn parties. When the school went on field trips to the symphony orchestra, Cynthia and I would ride together, so I knew her well. In the fall of 1963, she had just come to Ullman as a ninth grader. I was an eleventh grader, so I watched over Cynthia, sort of as my kid sister. She was only 14.

When I heard that Cynthia was dead, I was devastated. She was young and innocent. Then to add insult to injury, she had not even demonstrated. She had not gone to jail. I started to feel like they had killed the wrong Wesley girl, and had targeted me, but had gotten to Cynthia. I'm sure this doesn't seem to make sense; but I was a teenager with no life skill to handle thoughts of death. The details didn't sort well with me at that time. Now I'm a grandmother, and it all still haunts me.

The other names were released and the aching pain of familiarity struck again.

Carole Robertson was 14 and her father, Alvin Robertson, taught band at my elementary school and was my eighth-grade band teacher. **Denise McNair** was 11 and her father, Chris McNair, used to be our milkman with White Dairy Farms. He would deliver milk and orange juice to the house and I knew of Denise. **Addie Collins** was 14. I didn't know Addie personally; but that didn't change the gut-wrenching pain I felt. It seemed that everyone in our close-knit community was in some way connected to one or more of the girls. The pain seemed to fill the air; the community was in a state of emotional chaos.

September 15, 1963 was the longest day of my young life. The phone didn't stop ringing and my heart fluttered every time did. My parents and older siblings took the calls and I would hear them say repeatedly that it wasn't "our girl." Back then, the local telephone company published phone directory books for each city. Those books were an alphabetized listing of their customers that gave the home address and phone number. People were looking up the name Wesley in the phone book and since the Wesley options listed were few, our house was chosen many times that day. A lot of people at my school thought Cynthia and I were siblings anyway. There had been many Wesleys walking those school halls, and since they were all part of our family, it was reasonable to assume she was too.

I will always remember how sad and quiet our household was on that Sunday afternoon and evening. I don't remember a conversation being held in my presence, but I remember my mother being sad and upset. She did not sit down with me and say this could have been me or anything like that. We didn't have that kind of conversation. Perhaps the absence of words was out of fear of what was going to happen next. Mama talked with people on the phone, but they didn't share their thoughts and feelings with me. It was unusual for our parents to have conversations with other adults in our presence. That was probably why I didn't know a lot about mistreatments they had experienced, because that was never discussed openly with children present. They didn't talk about what happened to them. This bombing, as traumatic as it was to all of us, was no different.

As details emerged about the tragedy, we couldn't decipher truth from fiction. I heard that Cynthia's head had been taken off by the blast. I heard that Chris McNair found his daughter's shoe before he identified her body. I heard that Addie's older sister was summoned to the hospital; she thought she was to pick up her younger sisters, but it was really to identify Addie's body. I heard that Carole's mother wasn't ready for church and her daughter went on ahead to prepare to sing for the youth choir. I heard Mrs. Robertson had heard the noise of the bombing from their home and hurriedly made her way to the church. I "heard" a lot.

There were reports on the news and eventually, I was ready to listen. As I look back, it seems that our local news had shielded the more graphic details from view, perhaps for good reason, although that would never happen today. National magazines, like *Jet*, eventually carried the story in detail.

It was not uncommon for dynamite to be thrown into the yards of people who lived in what we called Dynamite Hill, a middle class, Black neighborhood in Smithfield. Many professional residents, including attorneys and educators moved to this area primarily as their White counterparts started to flee to the suburbs. They were often targeted by the Klan and it was not uncommon to hear an explosion of some sort coming from that area. It wasn't until the residents hired a White infiltrator to attend local KKK meetings did the bombings subside on Dynamite Hill. I heard that Mrs. Robertson had heard the explosion and had a sinking feeling that this was a different sounding blast for her.

That same day, September 15, two other Black Birmingham teenagers were also killed in a horrible manner. One was gunned down by a police officer who saw the young man running and thought he must have been involved in a rock-throwing demonstration. His name was Johnny Robinson, and he was only 16. The second was a thirteen-year-old boy riding the handlebars of his brother's bike. Two White teens returning from a Klan rally fired two shots to scare them. A bullet struck one of them and he tragically died. His name was Virgil Ware. That was life in Birmingham at the time but somehow the horror had never hit so close to home for me.

It's remarkable that we went to school the next day. We carried on as if all was okay, but it was clear that hearts were heavy. I don't remember any teacher suggesting that we sit down to talk about it. Counselors weren't assigned to seek out trauma and address it. I spoke with my peers in hushed tones among ourselves, but there were no official discussions to help us sort through our emotions.

I don't think I sensed anger, but I had a lot of questions as to why this had happened. How could someone do something like this? How could they throw a bomb into a church on a Sunday, knowing people would be inside? I eventually grasped the horrid, focused hate that had consumed those responsible. I further understood that this was just the beginning of more violent actions toward my community.

Carole Robertson's funeral was on September 17 and was a private family ceremony. The funeral services honoring the other three girls were held together at Sixth Avenue Baptist Church the next day. That church was located only about two blocks from my high school. I attended the funeral and sat in the balcony but I don't remember much of the speeches. I simply remember looking at those coffins and all the flowers, and internalizing all the moans and groans of the family members. I don't think I was able to adequately grieve over it. I was in shock. All those phone calls meant one thing to my young mind, that they had gotten the wrong Wesley girl.

Dr. Martin Luther King, Jr. was there and I remember seeing him speak, but I do not remember hearing him speak. His eulogy is readily available on the Internet, and revisiting it was quite moving to me. I had (and still have) a lot of respect and admiration for Dr. King, but in my day, he had not reached the level of popularity in the way we perceive him today. He was like any of the other well-dressed Black preachers I knew. I was familiar with our local ministers, Reverend Woods, Reverend Nelson, and Reverend Porter, among others. They were all well-respected, well-spoken, and well-dressed Black ministers, and I counted Dr. King among them. He could speak well and I knew what he was saying was important. I just could not focus on listening to him. That phone at home kept ringing in my head.

The atmosphere in the Black community was naturally grim and sober. People were horrified to think that someone could do this and there weren't any immediate arrests. We were all wondering who was going to be found responsible for this. When would an arrest come? After all, wasn't the killing of innocent children in church the ultimate sin against humanity? We heard that condolences and expressions of sympathy were coming in from all over the world, but somehow, we didn't feel the same sense of concern coming from within our own city. The question that seemed to be floating in the air was how could the world care and our own city not be concerned in the least.

Just a couple of months later, the community was still reeling from the church bombing and the lack of progress in the investigation when we received another shock. Our president, the man who had intervened and spoken on our behalf during the Children's Crusade, had been assassinated. Our president, who had sent one of his own men to come and help us, was dead. Our president, who was on our side and had said our treatment sickened him, was no longer with us. I watched the memorial services on television. Since this happened around the Thanksgiving holiday, we were allowed to stay up late to view the coverage.

When we got back to school after Thanksgiving break, President Kennedy's death was a topic for discussion in many of our classes, unlike the church bombing. It was all difficult to process. In one year, I had gone to jail, lost friends in a church bombing, and the President of the United States was murdered. The year 1963, for a long time, was difficult to discuss.

CHAPTER EIGHT

GETTING READY FOR THE WORLD

Once the tumult of the bombing and the assassination were behind me, I was well into my senior year, but had an unrealistic view of my future. It had been my life's ambition to become a teacher. I had so admired and respected my teachers growing up and wanted to walk in their footsteps.

I had seen something on television about UCLA in Los Angeles and I decided I would leave home upon graduating and attend there. Even though I had seldom traveled far from home and had no idea how I would pay for my education there, my mind was set on UCLA.

My high school guidance counselor was Reverend John Rice (father of former Secretary of State Condoleezza Rice). I never had a conversation with him about my educational future. He never sought me out and I never sought him out. I did not complete an application for admission or financial aid. With all of those siblings in my house and my parents working only low income jobs, I was naïve to think I was headed to Los Angeles.

I graduated in January of 1965 on a Sunday. My oldest brother, Henry, was enrolled at the time at Miles College, a small liberal arts school located here in Birmingham. He asked me on the Monday after graduation if I wanted to ride to the campus with him because he was registering for the second semester. I was out of school and didn't have anything else to do, so I went with him. We got to campus and I was greeted by a group of band members who promptly invited me to join. I told them that I was just accompanying my brother and wasn't a registered student. Henry immediately went to the college business manager to see about getting me registered.

Coincidentally, I had another brother, Alvin, who had

paid his application fee but did not attend because he joined the army instead. The business manager agreed to transfer Alvin's fee to me and advised me to complete the financial aid application. There I was at Miles College, with my brother helping me get registered at a local college, the day after I graduated from high school. The next day I was scheduled to take 15 hours of college classes and I joined the band to become a Miles College majorette. Alvin had volunteered and was sworn into the army the same day classes started.

I figured I could go to Miles until I went to UCLA, still living in an unrealistic daze. I didn't so much as have an application to UCLA. I had no money, and my parents couldn't afford to send me there. During our senior class day program, Mr. Bell, our principal, had chided the counselor, Reverend Rice, for not telling him about me. After all, I was in the top ten of my class and no scholarships had come my way. Mr. Bell lamented that had he known I existed, he would have referred me to his alma mater, Knoxville College, as he did many of his smarter students. Of course, I just smiled and thought to myself, it doesn't matter, I'm headed to UCLA.

My parents never said much about me going to Miles. My sister had graduated from Miles and was already teaching. Aunt Edith, with whom I had lived, was a Miles graduate. By then attending Miles almost a family tradition. It was probably expected that I would end up there more than I realized.

Attending Miles College wasn't a bad thing. A lot of the teachers I had in high school and elementary school had gone to Miles College. I got there, became part of the band, and embraced college life. Even though some signs of segregation were being slowly eradicated, I still attended an all-Black school, worshiped in an all-Black church, and lived in an all-Black community. Therefore, everyone I saw and dealt with on a regular basis was all-Black. The changes in society did not represent anything different for me personally.

Miles was in Fairfield, Alabama, a small town directly adjacent to Birmingham's west side. Founded in 1898 by a denomination called the Colored Methodist Episcopal Church, schools like Miles were desperately needed in the South since Black students were generally barred from attending White schools. These schools formed to serve the higher education needs of Blacks have come to be known as HBCUs or Historically Black Colleges and Universities. They still provide rich tradition and a sense of history to the African-American community today.

Unfortunately, many of the HBCUs are under tremendous pressure to compete with larger and better-funded institutions. Because these colleges represented our only hope for higher education, it's difficult for many to understand the loyal connection alumni maintain with those schools. I will be forever grateful for the service Miles College provided to my family and my community.

Miles did have an active exchange student program. We had one White student who was attending and took some classes with me. We had several White teachers, some from Ivy League schools. They had come to our little college to perform missions work to help the poor of the South. Regardless of why they were there, they represented what was my first interaction on any level with people of a different race. There were also a couple of African students enrolled there as well, which was also a new experience for me.

I became more aware of and involved with issues surrounding civil rights in college. Some significant leaders visited the campus. Stokely Carmichael, a Black activist who eventually become known as part of the Black Panther Movement and Party, came to the campus for a meeting. I would attend rallies on campus, but my focus was always on getting school work completed and trying to graduate. I majored in biology and minored in chemistry at Miles and pursued the required education courses to obtain the appropriate certifications to teach school.

When Dr. King was assassinated in 1968, I went with some friends to Atlanta to be a part of a memorial march. I couldn't get into the funeral, but participating in the march to the burial ground was a heartfelt experience that still resonates with me.

With all the deaths and assassinations in the U.S. along with the Vietnam War, there was a feeling that the world was upside down. I had many former classmates who were drafted and immediately sent over to fight in the Vietnam War. One of our neighbors, a young man named Bill Terry Jr., who lived a few blocks from us, was drafted. He told his mother that if he came home in a box, he wanted to be buried in Elmwood Cemetery, which was a big, beautiful cemetery near our home, but Elmwood was an all-White cemetery.

Unfortunately, Terry (as we called him) did come back in a box and when his mother went to make burial arrangements, she was denied. The NAACP and SCLC got behind the case and went to court. The KKK harassed his family throughout the judicial process. Elmwood was eventually forced to allow Terry's burial. Of course, by the time of the ruling, he had been buried in an all-Black cemetery. Terry was exhumed and there was another funeral and memorial service held for him. We marched from his church, Our Lady of the Immaculate Conception Church (now known as Our Lady of Fatima Church), to bury him in Elmwood. It's ironic that Elmwood is located right in the middle of an all-Black community, but Blacks weren't allowed to be buried there. In 1970, Terry became the first Black person to be buried there and I was honored to participate in that funeral processional march. By then, marching was something I had learned to do quite well.

I went to school during my summer breaks and graduated from Miles in three and a half years. I took a full load every semester while also working through the College Work Study Program (CWS), which is how I got through college. I graduated in the spring of 1968 and attended the University of Alabama at Birmingham to complete my student teaching. This was all I needed to acquire my teaching certification. My time at UAB was a unique experience for me. There were three other Blacks with me in a class with all White students. What a new world!

While at UAB, we took several tours to local schools, and

one was to Phillips High School. That was the first time I had walked into an all-White high school. It made me physically sick to walk on those steps that looked like they were marble, and see the thick velvet curtains in the auditorium. I looked in their art classroom where the students were taking a course called commercial art. It was amazing, to say the least.

At my high school, there was an art class, but they were using things like paper mache, nothing that could lead to an art career. We were taking classes like beauty culture or cosmetology and these White students were taking courses that were academically relevant and superior to what we were offered. I saw those three rooms of electric typewriters that had been mentioned in our prep meetings for D-Day. I looked in the bathrooms and saw the partitions, some that looked like they were made of granite or some other fancy material.

I was heartsick looking at all of that and reflecting on what my school had looked like. I was more than three years removed from high school, standing in a White high school and could see the differences I had never imagined existed. Even the furniture in their classrooms was different. When I looked at the size of their library, which was double the size of Ullman's, it made me angry and sad to think I had lived in Birmingham all my life and never knew the extent of the unequal conditions between Black and White schools. Seeing all that stirred up in me even more of a sense that it wasn't fair, and I was determined to see that things would be different as I moved into my educational career. Furthermore, I decided that if I ever had children, they would have access to the best education, and would be treated fairly.

As God would have it, when I graduated and completed the certification that summer, I was hired by the Birmingham School Board and was assigned to an all-Black school, Hudson Elementary. It was probably the largest Black school in the city and located in the middle of a large housing project in Collegeville. I had achieved my life's dream and was now a teacher. When I taught science in that school, I had twelve classes every day—alternating between six seventh-grade classes and six eighth-grade classes. Some students came Monday, Wednesday, and Friday, while some classes came Tuesday and Thursday. Some classes were for an hour and some were scheduled to run 45 minutes.

My lunch period was spent in the hallway monitoring and there were not enough textbooks for every child to have one, so they couldn't take the books home and had to do work in class. I had a demonstration table in the science room, but no equipment—not one microscope, test tube, petri dish, or anything close to lab equipment. I would go to my former schools, Miles College or UAB, and borrow equipment to demonstrate things to my classes. By now, you know what I was thinking: it just wasn't fair to our Black students to deprive them of the educational resources I knew the White students were enjoying.

At the end of that first year, I was summoned to the Board of Education, along with some other teachers, and was told I had been selected to go to an all-White school to teach the following year. They had handpicked qualified Black teachers so that Whites would know that we could do a great job. I went that fall of 1969 to an all-White school, McElwain. I taught seventh and eighth grade science and only had about four classes unlike the twelve I taught at Hudson. The students would come in the morning for instruction and in the afternoon for enrichment. I had a science lab, a demonstration table, and a closet with everything I could have imagined I wanted. I was told by the PTA president that if there was something I wanted that I didn't see, they would get it. The PTA was true to their word and I was blessed to have a fully-equipped classroom with everything I needed to enhance the learning experience for my students.

One of my students was the grandson of the first presidents of UAB, Dr. Joseph Volker. His mother, Virginia Volker, would bring loads of things that we could use for demonstrations and projects. My lunch period was duty free and I sat at a teacher's table where we were offered special lunch just for the teachers.

The difference between the two schools was like night and day. I couldn't believe I was in the same school system. Of course, there were also enough books for everyone. I was thrilled to have an opportunity to teach with so much support, but I was reminded daily that students and teachers back where I had gone did not have the same support.

The environment was not always pleasant. I would go into the office in the morning to sign in, and I would always say good morning. The principal wouldn't speak, the secretary wouldn't speak, and some of the teachers wouldn't greet me either. One of my Black friends, Lucille Lay, told me I was crazy to continue to go in and speak to those White folks when they didn't ever say one thing to me. I replied "I speak to that dog next door to me and he doesn't say anything either. I do it because it is the right thing to do." With that, I just kept on speaking every day.

There were two White teachers who had rooms on the same floor as mine who were very open to me. They helped raise my comfort level because they talked to me and embraced my being there. They gave me advice and information about how to be careful concerning my evaluations because people might want to see this project fail. I valued the friendships I had with Cora Walthall and Mary Jo Dean; they were the first White friends I ever had. The limited societal circle imposed on me was finally starting to expand.

Most of the children were quite open to me. There were a few who would try to make fun of how I pronounced a word as compared to how they pronounced the same word. If I was talking about a grassy area in front of my house, I would say, "My lawn is beautiful." One little boy came to me using his best southern accent, "that word is *lo-awn* not *lawn*." These negative exchanges were few and far between.

In my first days, a pretty little girl came to me after class one day in tears. She told me that some little boy in the class had called her a Jew. I asked if she was Jewish and she said yes. I asked why she was crying, and she said, "Well, that's like calling you a nigger!" and I said, "Oh, I see." I thought to myself, *I didn't know White people discriminated against other White people because of their religion!* My presence at the school was a learning process for me and it was pleasant 90 percent of the time.

It wasn't long before the children were receptive to me and they helped bring along their parents in the process. At first, I would not be notified in advance that parents would be coming to sit in my class to observe me teaching. When I tried to speak to the principal about it, he just shrugged it off. Consequently, I just started teaching the parents as if they were my students. I would call on Mrs. Jones and say, "We are looking at this atom, what part do you think this is?" Once embarrassed, they stopped dropping in.

Early in my tenure, some parents came to the school to have a meeting with me. Unprepared, I went to a conference room unaccompanied. I learned later the principal had the intercom on to listen to what was going on, but didn't provide me any support or notice that the parents were there to see me. The parents who came expressed their concern that I hated White people because my sister had been killed in the church bombing. It made me feel like that phone in 1963 was ringing all over again. Of course, I clarified that my sister had not been killed. I further explained that I knew the girl who was killed and she did have the same last name as I, but she was not my sister. I also informed them that I didn't hate White people. In fact, I told them I didn't really know any White people.

I was surprised that they knew anything about the Civil Rights Movement that had occurred a few years earlier, because by then it was 1969. I certainly didn't know they were aware of my involvement in the movement. It surprised me to hear them speak about something that happened in 1963; that wasn't anything anyone had talked to me about before. Another parent complained that I was teaching the students at a college level, however, most parents appreciated my advanced method of instruction.

While I was grateful for all that I had, it brought with it

some concerns. I remember thinking that this was so different, and I wondered how they were going to get a White teacher to leave this environment to go into the environment I just came out of. As I look back, most of the White teachers who went into Black schools were less prepared and were not the top teachers. I think the Black community lost something in that kind of transition because they took some of the best Black teachers and put them in White schools, but did not take the best White teachers and put them in Black schools.

I'm not implying that there were no qualified Black teachers left in the Black schools. They didn't select every great teacher and send them off to the suburbs. They did deprive the predominately Black schools of some of their better teachers, and I don't think they did the same kind of depletion with the White teachers going into the Black schools. It just wasn't quite fair, but I didn't know what the alternative was, for my presence was making a difference for my people, although my absence in the Black classroom came at some cost.

I also think that a skilled White teacher would not want to transfer into a Black area where they would be uncomfortable and unfamiliar. Those who did consent to go to one of those schools, who saw and felt the differences, probably weren't going to stay. I'm quite sure the Board had difficulty finding teachers who would go and stay in my community.

By the time I was preparing to get married in 1972, I had made many friends at that all-White school. Everyone's mother wanted to buy me a silver bowl or a dish or have a wedding shower for me. My new principal, Jack Mann and his wife Suzanne, even sang at my wedding. They were professional singers and didn't charge for their service as a gift to us. Several of my White friends attended my wedding.

In 1974, I was pregnant with my first child and everyone's mother wanted to give me a baby shower. I had so many clothes for my child, that she couldn't even wear them all. My world was surely changing.

I was at that school seven years, and the year that I left,

one Black student had finally enrolled. I transferred to West End High School, which had been the all-White school that my girlfriend had started attending and integrated in 1963. When I went there to teach after being at McElwain, West End was almost all Black. There were just a few White students there. Most of the White kids who lived in the West End community were attending church-schools. Many parents were pulling out of the public schools rather than have their children attend schools with people who looked like me.

I had always wanted to teach in high school. When I was a student, the Birmingham school system was set up with schools that ran from first grade through eighth and then high school from ninth grade to twelfth. Now, they were about to transition to a system that was kindergarten through fifth, middle school from sixth to eighth grades and then high school from ninth grade to twelfth. That would have meant that my school, McElwain, was going to be K through five, and I would have to leave. Since I had a secondary certification, I needed to depart and either go to a middle school or high school. When I was offered a position at West End High School, which was not very far from where I lived, I jumped at it.

I taught ninth grade physical science and twelfth grade physics. I was also the Student Government Association advisor and was heavily involved with many of the other activities at West End. Those were the most enjoyable years of my teaching career. When I left West End, I became a high school counselor, first at the alternative school for disruptive students and pregnant teens, and then at Woodlawn High (the same school where my mother had walked off her job). I was there for five years before I became an elementary school principal at Dupuy Elementary.

Through all my positions, I saw the system become segregated again, not by decree, but because of economics. Magnet schools were attracting high-performing students away from their neighborhood schools. Schools were being evaluated based on test scores and attendance records and students in the inner city were not performing well. We had buildings in disrepair. There was a big White flight to the suburbs. Those areas were less identified as a Black or White community, and there were a lot of Blacks moving into areas after Whites were moving out. Therefore, I saw rapid transitions in neighborhoods and school systems appear overnight, seemingly, within the small subdivisions.

In Birmingham, we now have thirteen independent school systems within a 20-25-mile radius of the downtown area. It is amazing how many different school districts have pulled away from the Jefferson County Schools and Birmingham City Schools to form their own, in order to gain more control over decisions and to limit access for others. I have also seen a lot of new construction in schools that are predominately Black schools, but our expectations for the students who attend are not as high as they once were. In these last few years I have seen a decrease in the professionalism of those who are teachers. When I graduated from college, we were taught that we had to dress in a certain way, behave in a certain way, and demand from our students so much more than what I saw in my last years of my teaching career.

I occasionally see students whom I taught during those years who share with me what they thought about being in my class. The general consensus is that they learned a lot, and admired and respected for me. They felt about me as I had felt for my teachers. It makes me feel good that I have poured into the lives of others, especially during such a time of inequality. It just wasn't fair, and I'm glad I was given an opportunity to do a little something about it.

we
thanks

CHAPTER NINE

CHURCH, FAMILY, AND CHURCH FAMILY

Once slavery ended, the Church was largely responsible for preserving Black lives and families, especially in the South. It was there that our people learned to read and write. It was the Church that we turned to for comfort and spiritual strength when injustices occurred such as a lynching, denial of justice in the courts, or being banned from the ballot box. At church, we could find peace and comfort in the Bible, the preaching, the music, and consolation of others who had gone through similar humiliations and experiences.

Many people attended churches that were in walking distance of their homes because they were poor and unable to afford vehicles to drive. At church, we met friendly faces who shared common interests and concerns. Church represented a place where there was a sense of equality before God, the equality that we were denied by many of our fellow White citizens. Life was predictable, and we felt that our churches represented a place of refuge. It was off limits to the acts of cruelty that we experienced in other public places.

That is why the bombing of 16th Street Baptist Church was so heinous and shocking to us, even before we knew of the casualties. The church belonged to us, was for us, and was run by us under God's watchful care. When someone invaded our sacred place where we could be free, we felt we had no retreat in this land of freedom.

I wondered how someone could place a bomb in a church on a Sunday? They had to know that it would be occupied and someone would be hurt. It bothered me to think that someone could be so evil.

I attended mass meetings at various churches, not my

home church, and I was very comfortable and felt excited to be present. The inspiring and upbeat music was engaging. There was no other place where Blacks could assemble themselves to talk about what was important to us.

The message I was receiving during those mass meetings was couched in terms that I could understand and that made sense to me. We sang a song, *God Is on Our Side*, and I believed that and internalized it. I was convinced that I was doing the right thing and that God was pleased with my actions. For me, that meant walking out of school, participating in the march, and going to jail were all ordained by God. I *still* believe that!

Church was an important part of who I was and who I am. After graduation, I became the youth director in my church. Since that time, I have served in many other capacities including Director of Christian Education, Sunday school teacher, and served in the deaconess ministry. Today, church and family are still at the center of my life. It's who I am and what I do. Currently, I work in an administrative capacity at my church where I am directly responsible for activities involving youth and community outreach, summer camp, after-school programs, and the child development center.

I was not disillusioned at any time with the Church as I watched the events of the Civil Rights Movement unfold. I was disappointed with how Christian people, especially some White people, would not accept us or acknowledge what was wrong with how Blacks were treated. The message in church was to love everyone and to "Do unto others as you would have them do unto you." How then could they be Christians and not feel remorse about how Black Christians were being rejected and treated? I was confused and disappointed that Black Christians and White Christians could not worship together.

I heard years ago there were people of color who attempted to enter a worship service at a large White church here in Birmingham, but were denied entrance. I wondered how they could justify keeping believers in Christ out of one of His churches.

Now more than fifty years later, change has come. My

church now partners closely with a predominately White church congregation. We serve cooperatively on mission projects, mission trips, and Bible studies, including Vacation Bible School. Our pastor preaches from time to time at their church and vice versa. We enjoy the cross-cultural experience and welcome each other at any time with open arms.

I have no plans to leave the church where I am a member, but I have seen a large migration of young Black professionals uniting with mega churches in this area that seem to be fully integrated. I think that is a sign of progress in the church.

Besides the Church, the family has always been the main institution in the Black community. For safety reasons and often by legal decree, the home was the focal point of life. Even in the home, children were often sheltered from the reality of life that parents faced. Children were not allowed in the conversations where adults discussed their treatment as second-class citizens. They covered up the pain of feeling helpless to do anything about it.

My aunt Edith, who taught for more than thirty years, retired and continued to serve her church as the organist. She fostered two daughters whom she later adopted. She had one biological son who was a graduate of Fisk University, Michigan State University, and Yale, where he retired as Department Head of Microbiology.

My parents had eight biological children, six boys and two girls. Another son became a member of the family in 1963. He was legally adopted several years later. Here is a quick overview of my siblings:

Elvia, my sister, is a graduate of Miles College and earned additional degrees from UAB. She retired after a successful career in education as a math teacher and counselor.

Henry attended Miles his freshman year. He began a career as a waiter in a supper club, which interfered with academics. Later, he was drafted and served in the U.S. Army. Upon his honorable discharge, he re-entered Miles and is currently a successful real estate agent.

William was the first of my brothers to serve in the Army. Following his honorable discharge, he was among the first Black men to serve in a supervisory role at the Birmingham Water Works.

Alvin initially enrolled at Miles College, and then opted out to serve in the Army. After his honorable discharge, he re-entered Miles College for two years when employment pulled him away and he eventually retired from the American Cast Iron and Pipe Company.

Charles first attended Texas Christian University before being drafted into the Army. After he was honorably discharged he worked as post master at Birmingham Southern College. While there, he took one class each semester until he completed his degree and earned his teaching credentials. He retired after twenty years teaching in the classroom.

John graduated from high school and was immediately drafted to serve in the Army. After a tour of duty in Vietnam, he returned home to battle post-traumatic stress syndrome. He trained at Lawson State Community College, where he earned a master craftsman certification in carpentry.

Michael graduated from Tennessee State University and later earned double master's degrees at Samford University and a Doctorate in Ministry. Because my mother had three sons serving in Vietnam at the same time, Michael was given a classification making him exempt from service. While pursuing a successful career in education (now retired), he became the senior pastor at Greater Shiloh Baptist Church, where he currently serves.

Gerald also attended Miles College and played basketball. He eventually became a master electrician.

My life took on new meaning when on July 8, 1972, I married a man I had known most of my life. He and I grew up in the same neighborhood church, South Elyton Baptist. His mother, Louise White Kelsey and most of her family, were longtime members of the historic 16th Street Baptist Church. Unlike me, Rufus had gone away to school on the West Coast, joined the army and stayed away from Birmingham for a while. Upon his return in 1970, we renewed our acquaintance and began dating. The rest is history!

After marriage I continued educational pursuits, earning a Master's Degree in Guidance and Counseling, then an Educational Specialist degree and certification in Administration and Supervision. In that span of time, we became parents to two children. Because my mother operated a daycare center, it was possible for me to work, go to school, and know that my children were well cared for.

As they became school age, we enrolled them in private, integrated Catholic schools. My unique experience with civil rights and teaching made me determined to give my children a well-rounded cultural experience. It was important to me to be sure they were exposed to the best that was available and were neither limited by the school zoning rules nor the color of their skin. Occasionally, they faced unpleasant experiences that I attributed to race, but not often. Each of them have formed lifelong, meaningful relationships with people of different races. My husband and I have encouraged them to embrace people based on their character.

My daughter, Katrice, is married and has three children. She is a graduate of UAB where she earned a master's degree in business administration. She is employed as an accountant for a non-profit organization. My son, Derrick, is also married and has two sons. Derrick graduated with a degree in electrical engineering from the University of Alabama (Tuscaloosa)—the same school where Governor Wallace stood in the door to prevent Blacks from entering. He also earned a degree from Dallas Theological Seminary. He currently works as an independent consultant and a missions pastor in Denver.

My husband retired from AT&T after 34 years of service. He served in the Army for ten years, served as president of our neighborhood association for twenty years, and is currently serving as church treasurer and deacon at South Elyton Baptist Church.

Church and family keep me centered. My siblings and I interact regularly and share holiday dinners together. Of course, we worship together as often as possible, most often at my current church where my brother Michael pastors. My son and his family live in Denver, and we are deliberate in planning time to spend together. With technology (mainly Facetime) we get to see each other and talk on a regular basis. My grandsons know that summer means coming to Alabama for two or three weeks to visit us and, yes, attend summer camp at church! Church will always center my family.

The day of the Black community has diminished and with that some of the values that we held dear have been lessened. I knew all the people in my community and they knew me. It was expected that community adults would discipline us if our parents weren't around at the time of the offense. That day is now gone. Although, I do not wish to return to those "good old days," I would desire to see a more cohesive, unified community such as I experienced when I grew up. With progress on some levels, there is also loss, but I don't want to go back to the way we were.

CHAPTER TEN

TELLING MY STORY

The first time I was invited to talk about my experience growing up in a segregated city, Mrs. Lillie Mae Fincher, a teacher at Hayes High School, asked if I would come to her class to talk about civil rights. My initial thought was that I was a science teacher and didn't know anything about civil rights. Mrs. Fincher had to remind me that I had gone to jail and had been among the first Black teachers in a White school. I prepared my talk and during my presentation, I started crying. Mrs. Fincher gave me a book that had a picture in it of me sitting on the floor in the Birmingham makeshift jail. At that moment, it seems I finally came to terms with the trauma that had been suppressed all those years.

That first presentation was probably around 1983. The next time I was asked to talk about it was in 1993. I was a counselor then and once again, Mrs. Fincher, who had become a supervisor at the Board over the social studies program, invited me. She contacted me along with some others who were also serving as educators and who had participated in the Children's March to come to Kelly Ingram Park to be interviewed by Board personnel preparing for a tribute about D-Day and other aspects of the Civil Rights Movement. My interview was chosen to be shown at the Board's meeting, and I was surprised that it got that kind of attention.

The next time I remember talking about it was when I was working at the Civil Rights Institute. I had retired from the Board in 2001 and started working at the Institute that year as the coordinator of a grant-funded program called Bridging the Gap. The program targeted at-risk children with the intent of keeping them from dropping out of school. Dr. Martha Bouyer, who was the coordinator for social studies for the Jefferson County schools, invited me to speak to a group of teachers in the building. Afterwards, she shared that the feedback had been extremely positive and encouraged me to find a way to share my story with more people.

After that, Martha was awarded a grant to invite teachers from across the U.S. to come to the Civil Rights Institute. She established *Stony the Road*, a historical tour of Birmingham, Selma, and other significant places. During the tour, the teachers talked about the Civil Rights Trail, the people involved, and the events that occurred. She once again invited me to speak to her group. I did speak and as had become my habit, I would break down when I got to the story of the 16th Street Church bombing.

The evaluations of my presentations were always quite high, and I started getting invitations from teachers attending those workshops to come to other cities to present. I got invitations to go to California, Hawaii, New York, Rhode Island, Texas, and Florida. I've gone all around the U.S. telling my story. Through these experiences, I was continually encouraged to put pen to paper and document my journey.

I have been interviewed on several occasions by people who were writing stories and accounts of the civil rights movement in Birmingham. Allen Zullo, a writer for Scholastic Inc., published a book in 2014 entitled *Ten True Tales: Young Civil Rights Heroes* and he featured my story. These positive encounters further prompted me to tell my story in my own way.

When I am invited to speak, I begin with a five-minute video clip showing some of the actual scenes of the Children's March where people were blasted by water hoses and attacked by dogs, along with a picture of 16th Street Baptist Church. After that, I begin my story. I tell the audiences at the age of 16, I didn't have civil rights on my radar screen. I was interested in dancing, being popular with my friends, and reading romance novels. I lived a typical teenage life. I didn't have any relationships with or fears concerning White people because I never encountered White people in my community. I guess we were all living in la-la land.

My parents didn't talk about race and I didn't know

any specific things that had occurred as it related to my family. I really was not aware of how bad things were for my people until I started going to those mass meetings. Then I talk about my decision to march, my arrest, and how my life changed from that point on.

Students always want to know if I got in trouble with my parents when I got out. They want to know if anyone failed to graduate because they marched. I've been asked why I decided to stay in Birmingham after going through that. The educators want to talk more about what it was like going into that White school and the differences between what it was like in the all-Black school versus the all-White school. Sometimes I am asked how to inspire youth to be more concerned and more responsive to current affairs.

I have remained in Birmingham because I've always lived here and I didn't have a reason to leave. I saw some positive changes that took place after I participated in the Movement. Some of the things I was protesting did indeed change for the better. I never wanted to leave because my family is here. Even after visiting other places, I saw some of the same kinds of situations that existed here. Moving probably would not have shielded me from the race war.

I always tell young people who want to be involved to stand up for what they believe in. I tell them that they don't have to be leaders or in charge of a movement to make a difference. They can make a difference within their circle, and not just about race issues. They can include those who are physically challenged as a way to make a difference, or befriend the kid who is being bullied. I stress that they don't have to be a part of putting someone else down because they're different.

I still have a goal of creating an awareness or continuing an awareness of human rights and not just civil rights. We are almost beyond the civil rights issue, although there are still problems that involve racial stereotypes and injustice. Where human rights are concerned, I want to help people open doors to dialogue that will help people get beyond their prejudices.

We cannot do that through legislation because we can't legislate love. We've got to find pathways to effective communication on so many levels so that we are not afraid of each other. A lot of prejudices people have are based on fear and inaccurate stereotyping. We move beyond that by stepping out of our box and talking to each other. This leads us to learning to appreciate the differences we may have. It also helps us uncover the fact that we generally are more alike than we are different. Yes, this is what I want to help make happen in my remaining time on earth.

CHAPTER ELEVEN

THE VIEW FROM MY SISTER'S SEAT

I thought it would be interesting to give two of my siblings a chance to provide their perspective on the events that led up to my arrest, and their interpretation of the impact the Civil Rights Movement in Birmingham had on them personally and on our family. We'll start with my sister Elvia, and then hear from my brother, Alvin, in the next chapter.

*****

My name is Elvia Lane and I live in Dixon, California where I have lived since 2000. Of course, I was originally from Birmingham, Alabama, but after my husband died, I remarried and moved to Dixon. I have been asked to share what I recall about Janice's involvement in the events of May 1963 that led to her arrest.

In the early '60s, I began working as a teacher, teaching math at Hayes High School in Birmingham for grades nine through twelve. As you know by now, the marches with the children involved youth from high school. We teachers had heard what they were considering, and we were advised that we could not force them to stay in class. If they chose to leave, then they would be free to do so. That was generally the approach in many of the schools, but certainly it was the rule in my class and school. I concluded that kids would rather march than do geometry or algebra with someone whom they considered a hard teacher like me, so I was resolved to the fact that my students were going to march. During the period of days when the marches occurred, I may have had four or five kids in class and in some of my classes, there were none.

As far as my family was concerned, we had no real thoughts about the demonstrations prior to Janice going to jail.

I was impressed that the youth were marching and that something was being done in my home city to protest the treatment we were receiving. I remembered all too well the Montgomery Bus Boycott started by Rosa Parks in 1955. Soon after the news reached us about what was going on in Montgomery, we had the same situation in Birmingham. Blacks in general decided not to ride the Birmingham bus system in support of Rosa and the people in our capital city.

In the part of the city where we lived, there had been a special bus that picked up kids along the way and drove them the one mile or more to school. When that bus would pass during the boycott, however, it was almost empty. As kids, we enjoyed yelling at the buses and telling them we didn't want or need a ride. That meant we just walked or someone drove us to where we were going. There were also adults who also chose not to ride, and there were jitneys (cars that served as unofficial cabs) that would pick people up and give them a ride to downtown for a minimal fee. By and large, Birmingham joined with Montgomery in the bus boycott.

Prior to the bus boycott, we were riding the buses where there was a placard that said "White" on one side and "Colored" on the other side. The driver or White riders could take that placard and put it wherever they chose. Once the sign was in place, Blacks would have to sit behind that placard. We lived in an area that was predominately Black, so often half of the bus was open to us. People who lived closer to White neighborhoods had few if any seats and had to stand. Even if there were open seats in the White section, Blacks were not allowed in those seats.

When civil unrest came to Birmingham in 1962 and 1963, I didn't know Janice was involved one way or the other because she didn't say anything about it. I did know that the civil rights meetings were held in the evenings at the various churches. I understood as a first-year teacher and as a teacher in general that if we were involved and were arrested, we would lose our jobs. So therefore, I was not involved in any of the mass meetings. That is why the strategy was to use youth in the protests since many of the adults were threatened and intimidated not to protest.

When the yellow busloads of kids who had been arrested would pass near the house, we could hear them singing and they would yell out to us as they passed. I stood with my mother and we waved at the kids on their way to jail or to Fair Park where the children were held.

When I came home from work on the day she was arrested, I discovered Janice had taken my leather jacket with her to jail. My dad discovered she had taken the toothpaste, which meant everyone was scrambling the next morning without any. I later told her that after high school, when she got a job, she needed to replace my jacket! That replacement has yet to happen. Losing my leather jacket was the price I had to pay for her marching.

I knew that the Children's Crusade was significant, because we had grown up in a segregated society where everyone looked like us no matter where we went—school, at social events, or church. That meant there was not a lot of interaction between Black and White people. The Crusade for the Civil Rights Movement in general brought those issues to light, and people began to challenge what had been accepted in the South and especially in Birmingham for generations. Because of the marches and the things that Commissioner Bull Connor did in response to the marchers, such as releasing dogs on the kids and spraying them with water hoses, I began to resent and dislike White people and I had not even had any physical contact with them one way or the other.

When I came to learn that my sister was one of those arrested and in jail, I was concerned about what was going on because we heard a lot of rumors. We heard that the officials were not treating them fairly and that they were without proper food. Those reports turned out to be rumors, but nevertheless it caused me and especially our mother to worry. A report had gotten out that someone was sick, so then she worried that it was Janice who was sick. I wanted Janice to be safe, but I didn't fear she was in danger. I knew my mother wasn't so convinced.

I was surprised when I first heard that Janice had participated, but then again, she was always one to get involved in things, probably more so than I. She had an energetic personality about anything going on. If there was an issue, Janice would be somewhere in the middle of it. By contrast, I wouldn't normally even know about things going on in the community. When I look back and think about her personality, I should not really have been surprised. The march and demonstrations would have been appealing to her much more than they would have appealed to me.

I was pleased with the results that we saw in Birmingham after the youth marches. There was a learning curve that we had to deal with because eventually, as of a result of the protests, schools were also desegregated. They took some White teachers and brought them to the Black schools and took some teachers in the predominately Black schools and moved them to White schools. For the first time, I worked alongside of Whites who were also teaching.

I found there was a difference in the way we approached students. Some of the White teachers seemingly felt it okay to refer to these teenager boys as boys, and the young men resented that. Generally, we referred to them as young men. When a White teacher addressed a Black youth and said, "Boy, get out of the hall!" Instead of the student responding and obeying because an adult had spoken to them, they would respond negatively and say, "I'm not a boy; I'll show you what a boy is." For the most part, it created bitterness and resentment. There was no way we could explain to the White teachers how insulting it was to be referred to as boy, so a lot of ill feelings got pushed below the surface where they lingered and festered.

For some reason, that mattered a lot to the White teachers. They seemingly wanted to hear "yes ma'am" and "no sir" and the kids were not willing to say that. It was just a cultural thing and I think those things had to be worked out, even among the teachers themselves. Some of the Black male teachers felt freer with some of the female teachers, saying something like "Hey baby, how you doin'?" That did not have a sexual connotation, but of course White women did not want to hear a Black man say, "Hey girl, how's it going?" It didn't mean anything to me, it was simply someone speaking, but the White teachers felt they were being treated disrespectfully. We had to work through some of those things and we had to attend workshops to help us deal with those issues.

I think we all felt there we were making progress in overcoming segregation until the 16th Street Church bombing the following September. I was incensed and angry, as was all the Black community. The bombing touched all of us in some way, and it was particularly painful for me because Claude Wesley, Cynthia's father, was one of my fellow teachers at Ullman. Alfa Robertson, Carole's mother, was the librarian at Hayes High School. Her husband, Alvin Robertson, had been the band teacher at Washington Elementary School. Though I was not in the band, I did know Mr. Robertson. I heard Mrs. Robinson speak years later about how angry he was and how he resented the fact that his daughter was killed. I truly empathized with how he felt.

I knew Chris McNair, Denise's father. At that time, he was the delivery man for White Dairy, and delivered to our home. Even though I did not know the families personally, I knew of them and we were part of a community that had banded together because of segregation. Therefore, I grew ever more resentful because of the bombing and the lives that were lost. Around that time, there were always homes being bombed. We would hear a bomb go off on Center Street, which was a few blocks from where we lived. Or we would hear of a bomb on Center Street North and Tenth Court, which was a nice neighborhood that was mostly Black. The Klan and their friends were just bombing homes, not churches. Therefore, the church bombing was a total shocker. I did not at all like that, and I did not at all like White people because of it. I knew some of them were not involved, but they were all in one category as far as I was concerned, and that was the category of hateful enemies. I thought it was awful and wondered what would cause people to do such a thing.

We all watched Governor George Wallace spew his racist venom everywhere and we were powerless to stop him. I'm sad to say at the time my faith was not as strong as it has come to be. I felt when he was shot and paralyzed, it was payback for some of the ugly things he had said and done. I did not feel very sympathetic towards him at the time the incident happened. That's what happened throughout our state—people became alienated from one another.

Wallace uttered during his campaign the famous phrase, "segregation today, segregation tomorrow, segregation forever." I remember him standing in the door at the University of Alabama to prohibit Blacks from entering, and I thought, *How dare he do that.* One of my joys was when I had the opportunity to go to the University of Alabama. I took summer classes there and I thought, "Well, this isn't such a big deal after all."

The fact that he stood in that schoolhouse door and I was not allowed to attend there made me angry and resentful. When I got a chance to attend, I went, as if to say, "Now what do you have to say?" My mother was working for a doctor at the time, and he explained to her that integration would happen, but not in our lifetime. The summer I went to Alabama, I went straight to that doctor for my physical so he would know that it was happening in his lifetime, because I was going!

I think if I had been a few years younger, perhaps I would have participated in those marches and protests. At 22 years of age, my focus was on my new career. As a matter of fact, when I was attending Miles College, we did have some demonstrations on campus. Some of the guys were quite vocal about what was going on. Therefore, the Crusade was not the first time I had heard or seen protests about some of the discriminatory actions. For that reason, I did feel a lot of resentment.

When Janice was chosen for the pilot project to teach in an all-White school, I was very proud of her. She had finished school and started teaching right away, and within a short period of time she was sent to a predominately White school and made friends with her coworkers there. Her colleagues liked her and her bubbly personality and she liked them. I was proud of the fact that she could make that kind of adjustment. I was leery of their actions, and I observed the interactions with an eye of suspicion, but I was proud of her.

Janice was a good teacher, and I would have put her up against any other teacher in our city's system. I don't think they had any others, Black or White, who were any more qualified or dedicated than she was. Therefore, I had no reservations about her role and her ability to be professional as she carried out that role.

When the Civil Rights Institute opened in Birmingham, I thought it represented an element of education that had been lacking for many years. We are not taught to respect the contributions of Blacks to our society. We were not taught what individual Blacks had done and we were just generally made to feel like second class citizens. The opening of the Birmingham Civil Rights Institute highlighted all that our people had gone through, particularly the emphasis on the fight for voting rights. It helped me and others who had not been so close to the effects of segregation and the Civil Rights Movement see and know that Blacks have made significant contributions to our city and country. I thought it was one of the best things that could happen so that the next generation could look and see all the things we had to live through.

Youth today always ask: You really had to ride buses in a separated fashion? You really could not eat in a restaurant because of the color of your skin? Until the protests of the Civil Rights Movement, people had not been forced to face the realities of how we were treated.

All that made me angry, but we had to be careful not to show our anger. We were told to be patient, that things were improving, but they were not improving that quickly until the protests. I felt anger and resentment that it was not right then and it still isn't right in a lot of instances today. Yes, relationships are better between the races, but all isn't right. Though I live in a very different society, there is still a lot of room for improvement because I still see vestiges of segregation attitudes among some people.

I hope this book will give some insight into what life was really like for us growing up. Some people look at Blacks, having not had any experience with segregation, and tend to say they think they know how we feel. No, they don't really. They have no idea how I feel, because they have never had to endure these kinds of injustices. I now have Caucasian friends, and they really are dear friends of mine. As a matter of fact, I have a Caucasian friend, about my age, who calls herself my twin, even though she is half my size. We share good laughs and fellowship.

There was a time I never would have thought I would have had this kind of a relationship with someone of a different race. Even so, I know she cannot really understand a lot of what I say or think. I like the multi-cultural church I attend very much and we are kind of like a family. When my White counterparts start to talk about our president-elect (now President Trump) and how he is their choice, they don't really understand why I would have strong feelings about that. One time in a discussion I realized that they really don't get the subliminal messages he sends to his admirers. That made me realize that I still have some bitterness. My maturity has taught me how to better process those feelings. I've come a long way and much of that can be attributed to my spiritual growth.

The Children's Crusade took courage and that courage spread to many other groups. While Blacks protested in the '60s, many groups now take to the streets or the Internet to say, "This isn't right." I would like to think that my sister was at the forefront of that social phenomenon. As I look back, I am proud of her role and her ongoing role in Birmingham to bring attention to injustice past and present. I know that writing this book will enable her to tell her story to even more people. My hope is that they will understand what it was like to live in the segregated South and what it was like to be a part of a historic protest that was part of a larger, powerful Movement. I guess losing my jacket wasn't such a high price to pay.

CHAPTER TWELVE

THE VIEW FROM MY BROTHER'S SEAT

My name is Alvin Wesley and let me start by making it clear that my two sisters were both educators, and I can't communicate as much or as well as they can. Having said that, in May of 1963 I was in high school and playing football for Ullman High. We were practicing and having spring training when the civil rights protests started in Birmingham and many of my friends got involved. At first, I didn't want to have anything to do with it. We were told that if we missed practice, we would not play in the fall games; and I really wanted to play.

I did manage to go to a couple of mass meetings with Janice. Some of the civil rights leaders were there telling us how badly we were being discriminated against; that we were getting White leftovers for school books and athletic equipment. I knew that because I was playing football and we would get old equipment from other White high schools. We would paint the helmets with our school colors, which were green and grey. We would take their old football cleats home and shine them up. I knew what they were saying was true.

When Janice was arrested, my mother was upset because of all the rumors going around, some of them true and some not. As Janice's oldest brother and a football player, I thought I was pretty in touch with what was going on. Then it hit me that Janice was in jail, and here I was a big-time football player, and I was not in jail. I needed to get involved!

The Monday after Janice was released, our mother admonished me to "go to school." I promised her that I was on my way to school, but I really wasn't. Our school was on the south side and 16th Street Baptist Church was on the Northside. I headed right for the church. In the church, it seemed like a big pep rally. Everyone was out of their seats, clapping, singing, and crying, and before I knew it, I was in the mood. We marched out of church in pairs and I was holding hands with some cute girl I had never seen before. We walked out singing. At the porch we were met with a line of dogs, policemen, and news reporters. It was a frightening scene. We kept going and marched about a half block before we were stopped for violating the city code. We were told the same as Janice and her group had been told. Get out of line and there will be no repercussions; if not, go to jail. Everyone in line stayed put. This was May 6.

Janice was arrested on a Thursday and the jails were full after that initial group was processed. Jail space was limited and the police tried to discourage us by using the water and dogs. I witnessed all of that, but I didn't get hit with the water or attacked by the dogs.

When I was arrested, I was put in a paddy wagon just as Janice had been. We had at least twice as many people inside as the wagon was designed to hold and we went straight to the city jail. When we got there, the jail was full and we had nowhere to go, so we stayed out in the yard for a few hours until they made arrangements.

The jail experience was almost fun because all my friends were there. There were people I went to church with, to school with, and people who just lived in the community. I wasn't afraid at all, and I was not personally mistreated. We had to stand in line when we went to lunch and dinner, and we had to be quiet when we were sitting at the table. I was in from that Monday until Friday. While I was there, I did see an incident that gave us all reason to be mindful of how we behaved.

We were at breakfast and the school kids were sitting around complaining that the grits were cold, the bacon was cold, and the toast was cold. One of the guards smacked the table and told us to shut up or he was going to put everyone out. The comedian Dick Gregory was in there with us by then and he said to the guard that he couldn't tell anyone to shut up, not even his wife. When he said that, two policemen grabbed Dick

Gregory and dragged him out of the mess hall. When we saw Dick Gregory again, his whole face and his suit were bloody.

I was not really surprised that Janice participated, because Janice wanted to be involved in just about everything and the protests were something many of the school kids were doing. I was concerned for her with so many rumors out that kids were sleeping on the cold floor or they didn't have enough food to eat. When she came home, I knew it was my turn to do my part and get involved. Her participation stirred me to action.

There were some noticeable changes in Birmingham after the protests and I guess we all felt things would keep getting better. Then the incident at the church took place the following September. The 16th Street Church Sunday morning bombing was a horrible event. I had worked with my father at a nightclub that Saturday night before, so we got home late that Saturday night or early Sunday morning. I was in bed asleep when I heard the blast go off. It shook the house a good bit and I thought, "Oh my God, what was that?" I tried to go back to sleep.

A few minutes later the phone began to ring because one of the girls killed was named Cynthia Wesley and people were calling wanting to know if it was one of our Wesley girls who had been killed. It was common knowledge that at least one of our Wesley girls would have been in Sunday school at that time. I got up, put my clothes on, and went to our church. Seeing my mother and sister gave me great relief. I was truly sorry about the other children who were killed, but I was relieved that it wasn't one of my sisters.

Our White politicians did not serve the interests of our Black community and catered to White audiences and voters. In fact, not many of my people could vote, so the officials had no incentive to serve our interests. That is in part why we protested. We had to take matters into our own hands. Our governor at the time of all this was George Wallace, and I thought George Wallace was a racist, pure and simple. I felt that anyone who drove around with George Wallace bumper stickers was also a racist. I knew he would do or say anything to the White community to stir the pot. At that time, segregation was what they wanted, and that's what he stood for.

Right after the civil rights protests, I went into the army. When I came out, I could really see the difference and changes in my city. I felt like all that the people had done and gone through was worth it. I felt proud that I was a part of it. While I was in the army, White recruits had their own attitudes about Blacks and we had our own attitudes about Whites. We all slept in the same barracks and learned to live together. Some of the Black guys from the North wanted to know how we could put up with what was going on down South, because it was all over the papers. They knew the police had used the dogs and the fire hoses on the school kids. They were curious about how things were.

When I got out of the Army, I went to work at a pipe plant. I went to Miles College for a few years, but then I stopped and started working full-time. As I look back, I see that society is so different now. Back 50 years ago, there were no Black bus drivers, Black policemen, or Black city council people. There were no Black people in city hall, period.

My two sisters ended up as educators. I am proud of them both. Janice and I used to discuss the differences she found between the White schools and the Black schools. We had been in high school together at the same time, so I understood what she was saying and seeing; I understood all that the White schools had that we did not.

I was glad to know that the truth was coming out that there was a difference, which we all suspected had existed. I always wondered why the White schools test scores would be higher than ours. She talked about the learning opportunities the White students had, and they were totally different from Blacks. That's why the White schools test scores were higher; it was because they were exposed to so much more in the learning experience.

When I first visited the Civil Rights Institute in Birmingham, I felt real close to some of the things I saw. I saw pictures of the police dogs and the little girls marching, and they were all things I had witnessed with my own eyes. I recalled that it took three men to control the force of the water from those hoses that they sprayed on the children. In fact, Bull Connor had wanted to increase the pressure, but the firemen refused to do it. When I saw videos of those girls rolling on the ground and being washed down the street like you wash leaves or pine straw out of your driveway, I got angry and it became personal for me all over again. It makes me sad that we had to go through as much as we did to get where we are now. We as a people are not all the way there, but things are so much better.

As young people read this book, I hope they will understand the life they live now is a result of the courage of others. My daughters have opportunities that my siblings and I didn't have. I hope my people realize that they have been blessed in the past by people who had the courage to stand. They had the courage to stand in front of dogs, nightsticks, and in front of people saying they would not be able to get a job if they got involved, but they stood anyway. I hope they will understand the courage and bravery it took to do that.

In the '60s, my mother had five boys go into the United States Army. Three went to Vietnam. As a family, we have served our country; several of my siblings have served the local community as educators. That makes me proud. I salute Janice for documenting the legacy.

****

I think my brother and sister have expressed how we felt being born into and living in a segregated society. At first, we didn't pay much attention because that was just the way it was. We had accepted it as life in the South. When it was brought to our attention that some of this stuff was unfair, pure and simple, and we were presented with the opportunity to do something about it, I for one was all for it. I said, "Let's go. Let's get it on!" I think my entire family had that feeling, whether they expressed it back then or not.

I had never heard Elvia express her feelings of bitterness about what happened back then. She is a relatively quiet, reflec-

tive person, but it made me feel good to know that they both thought well of my participation. As my brother and sister said, we are not where we need to be, but we are a long way from where we were.

BM

27054

ALVIN WESLEY Deft. 37 South 3rd Avenue Court No.

Charges 1. Violation Section 1159 GCC

R. C. No. 76653-J Convicted in R. C. June 13, 1963 Jury Yes

Fine $ 100 Costs $ 5 Days 180 Days suspended Driving suspended days

Arresting Officers D. W. Dailey

Bondsmen Reliable Bail Bond Services by M. W. Ryles

Bond $300 Attys. for Deft. Shores and Billingsley

NAME OF WITNESSES AND ADDRESSES WC DC

Settled Through City Attorney's Office for Dollars,

which amount was paid 19 Cashier's Receipt No.

MISCELLANEOUS

3-17-69 [illegible] FILED IN OFFICE

JUL 3 0 1963

[illegible] SWIFT

CLERK

Arrest Record of Alvin Wesley (we have been unable to locate mine)

DATE 5-6-63 TIME 1:40PM PLACE ARRESTED 5 ave. 17 St. No. CHARGE Sec. 1159

NAME Alvin Wesley SEX M COLOR B AGE 17 DATE OF BIRTH 12-15-4[illegible]

ADDRESS 37- 3 ave. So.

PARENTS NAME(OR GUARDIAN) Henry Wesley ADDRESS Same

SCHOOL Carver GRADE 12 gr. WHERE EMPLOYED —

TEACHER'S NAME Keny

ARRESTING OFFICERS D. W. Dailey INTERROGATING OFFICERS J. B. Frommell [illegible] Donaphe

PLACE OF INTERROGATION City Jail

WE AS INTERROGATING OFFICERS INFORM YOU OF YOUR RIGHTS THAT ANY STATEMENT YOU MAY MAKE MAY BE USED FOR OR AGAINST YOU. KNOWING THIS DO YOU WISH TO MAKE A STATEMENT? no

CHURCH AFFILIATION South Elyton Baptist MEMBER yes REGULAR: YES( ) NO (✓)

ARE YOU A MEMBER OF A.C.M.H.R., S.C.L.C. OR OTHER ORGANIZATION? YES( ) NO (✓) NAME OF ORGANIZATION TO WHICH YOU BELONG

WHERE DID YOU MEET TO ASSEMBLE? 16 St. Baptist Church

WERE YOU AWARE THAT THERE WAS AN INJUNCTION PROHIBITING THE ACT THAT YOU WERE ENGAGED IN? yes

WHO BRIEFED YOU ON ACTIONS TO TAKE? Don't know

WHERE DID THIS BRIEFING TAKE PLACE? 16 St. Baptist WHEN? 11AM

WHAT OTHER OFFICIALS WERE PRESENT AT BRIEFING? Don't know

WHAT WERE YOU INSTRUCTED TO DO? ~~[illegible]~~ March

DO YOUR PARENTS KNOW THAT YOU WERE TO PARTICIPATE? no.

DID YOU LEAVE FROM SCHOOL? Didn't go today WHAT TIME DID YOU LEAVE —

WHAT IS THE "PEACE PONY"? Don't know

WHAT IS THE "UNTOUCHABLES"? Don't know

REMARKS:

CHAPTER THIRTEEN

A MARCH OF A DIFFERENT KIND

I'd felt a lump in my breast back in the fall of 2010. I had told my personal physician, and I was sent to the breast clinic. They examined the lump and diagnosed it as a complicated cyst, something that usually went away in the same way it showed up. My doctor and internist told me I didn't need to worry about it since it was too big to be cancer. The breast clinic told me I needed to come back in six months to have it looked at again, and when I went back, it was not gone.

Three days after going in, I got a call from the doctor while I was working at the church. The woman on the phone asked if I was alone. She then asked me if I could come back with my husband the next day to see the doctor. I sat down and inquired further. She told me they had found two cancer cells. My husband and I went in the next day to talk and look at the x-rays.

After they did a second mammogram in 2011, they tried to draw the fluid off. They had done those incisions before. They couldn't get a needle through it because it had hardened. They decided to remove it and three days later I got *that* call. They found stage one cancer cells and apparently, they had not gotten all of it when the original lump was removed, because at that time they didn't realize cancer was involved. It was an aggressive form.

Three weeks after the first surgery, I had the second. I thought everything was okay and went back to work after couple of days and got a call again. I went back the next day and the doctor explained that no cancer cells were found in my lymph nodes, however there were cells found in the tissue and another surgery was needed. I went back for the third surgery and had a lumpectomy. The surgeon scraped all the way to my breast bone and there were no new cells found. The recommendation, however, was for me to have chemotherapy and radiation. I received a year of chemo, followed by 35 consecutive days, except for weekends, of radiation.

My maternal grandmother, who passed away before I was born, died of breast cancer. My mother's sister, Aunt Lucille, had died of breast cancer. Obviously, I was always concerned about the possibility of having it. When I would go to the doctor, I always made sure they knew I had this history. To be faced with the reality of having cancer, was a traumatic experience.

My support system was incredible. My husband went with me to every treatment. Some of them lasted for hours and he would sit in clinic with me until I fell asleep. He would then go to the waiting room until it was time to go home. He was there with and for me 100%. My family, and my sister especially, who lives in California, would call and write and send me things. She would send booklets, pajamas, and other gifts. I would struggle to go into work at the church and she would have sent flowers or a fruit bowl. I was bound and determined not to give in to cancer. Often, I would show up to work at the church and stay until they sent me home. This was certainly a march of another kind; and yet it was still a fight for freedom.

I started writing every week that I would go for treatment. I wrote a personal blog on my experience and sent it to certain members of the family. That helped me get through it.

This (2016) is my fifth year being cancer free. I've been monitored closely and don't have to see the doctor for a year from our last visit. I lost all my hair and lost a lot of weight, which I wish I could have kept off, but it came back. I guess the worst part about it, other than not feeling well, was being tired all the time. Generally, I'm very active; I like moving around, doing things, and walking every morning; it took that away from me. I still haven't gotten back to being as physically active as I was accustomed to being.

I think the Lord intended for me to use this as a ministry to help others; to serve as a living testimony as to what He can do. I'm able to witness to others about His saving grace. I can tell people of His power to heal. I am very encouraged by that, because I have shared my testimony many times with other women who've gotten *that* call. Others are often amazed when they learn that I had cancer. They often say, "you don't look like you've been through all of that." I hope I have served as an inspiration to other people who battle their own illnesses or who have loved ones battling. Don't sit down. Don't lie down. Keep on marching!

CHAPTER FOURTEEN

IT'S STILL PAYING OFF; MY FINAL SPIEL

As we discussed in earlier chapters, my city of Birmingham figured prominently in the Civil Rights Movement that impacted America and the world. At some point, cities like Birmingham began to look for ways to chronicle and memorialize the journey as citizens pursued social justice and equal rights. One of the ways that municipalities determined they could best do this was to erect monuments, museums, and libraries to commemorate the events like the Children's Crusade.

In 1979, Birmingham's then mayor proposed a civil rights museum for our city. That was exciting enough and then, a Black gentleman by the name of Richard Arrington, Jr., ran for mayor later in 1979 and was elected. Many of us never thought we would see the day when a Black mayor would preside over our divided city.

Mayor Arrington picked up on the idea of a civil rights museum and plans were put together but no funding was available. It wasn't until 1986, when Mayor Arrington expanded the task force for the founding of a museum, that the idea took on new life. Eventually, the project was funded by state and local money, and on November 5, 1992, the Birmingham Civil Rights Institute opened its doors. Today, I am honored to serve on its board of directors.

I was excited that a building would be erected to house information and preserve the history of the Civil Rights Movement, and especially those aspects that occurred in Birmingham. Up to that point, it was history that had not been talked about very much. Now when I walk through those doors, I relive some of my history, and it still becomes an emotional experience sometimes. The Institute has many displays that tell the story of Birmingham, its history of segregation, and its attempts to establish justice. There are old television sets that show the national news broadcasts reporting what was happening in Birmingham, including the Children's Crusade. Seeing those reports takes me right back to being arrested.

I surprised myself when I first saw the displays. I had not really been confronted back then with what had happened because I was in jail. What happened was seldom discussed or talked about. Seeing it unfold before me in this "safe zone" was very painful, and yet liberating. Going further on in the Institute, I had to look at the pictures of the church bombing and read the reports about what happened to the bodies of the young girls. The 16th Street Baptist Church where the bombing took place is across the street on the north side of the Institute. Kelly Ingram Park, where the dogs attacked and the hoses were unleashed, is also across the street to the east of the Institute. As difficult as it can be to view the displays repeatedly, I appreciate the investment in the preservation of this vital history.

The Institute is looking forward to a future where it will not only preserve history, but will play a relevant part by being a source of information about racism and the ongoing battle to remove its effects from our country. We hope to continue to not just talk about what happened, but to also offer solutions and a means to reconciliation. We must find ways to open conversations between people while we remind people of the past. This is the surest way, I think, that we not repeat that horrible time and place in history.

Being chosen to serve on the board brought me full circle. From being a child marching in a monumental movement to serving on the board of directors for the Institute, entrusted to protect the legacy of that movement. I've come full circle, and I'm proud to have served then and now.

I have been to memorial services for the church bombing, the most recent being the fiftieth anniversary in 2013, which was quite a large event. Dr. King's daughter attended, Andrew Young was there, and many others came to 16th Street Baptist

Church to remember. At that time, special statues were erected in Kelly Ingram Park to commemorate the four girls who died in the church bombing. I stood there and cried as I reflected on the pain and suffering encountered and the human cost paid to see progress made in race relations in this country. I also wept because we aren't where we should be, and we have a long way to go.

I sat in a church recently and listened to the Carlton Reese Memorial Choir. That mass choir isn't nearly as large as it was when the 1963 mass meetings were being held on a regular basis. In fact, they don't even call themselves a mass choir anymore. They sang familiar freedom songs, and some in the choir were the same men and women who sang in the '60s choir. I reflected on how much those songs meant to me and how they helped me decide that protesting was the right thing to do. There is true power in the message of the music. So much so, that before making a presentation at school in New York, I was forced to leave the auditorium and collect myself as they played the song, *I'm on My Way to Freedom Land*. The lady that led the song in the '60s, Ms. Mamie, can still be heard today singing the song for different occasions around the city. The music was such an important part of the Movement, and it still stirs deep feelings in those of us who participated in the protests.

The two elections of President Obama felt like true progress. It felt like we had indeed overcome, and that Black and White people had come together. I was glad we were finally on the right road and our sacrifices were not in vain. When I listened to President Obama take the oath in 2008, it was significant in so many ways. About 20 of my family members were in attendance with me and as luck would have it, one of my brothers and I were smitten enough to stop and take a selfie with a cardboard image of the president-elect. We ended up getting separated from our group on what seemed to be the coldest day in history!

We took the Metro train back to the hotel and watched the ceremony in the warmth of the hotel lobby with some good chicken fingers while our family was out there braving the cold.

The many who were in the lobby cheered, and strangers were crying and hugging. It was a joyful experience to be a part of. I also traveled to Washington for his second inauguration, but it was a smaller group of family members who went with me. This time, my niece had a connection and having VIP seats was a great comfort; no chicken fingers that go 'round.

Our most recent election in 2016 brings with it some concerns regarding race relations. For me personally, some of the recent rhetoric reminds me of George Wallace and the speeches he gave. Governor Wallace got crowds excited through divisive messages, and I'm seeing those same messages coming again through our nation. My hope is that the Civil Rights Institute will be a relevant fortress as we continue to work through the race relations we now face. We must find a way to continue to bridge racial gaps.

As I conclude my story, I admit that it's been painful for me to acknowledge that I didn't recognize I was being treated so poorly when we were growing up. I was insulated from some of the harmful limitations. When I look at our Black community, I see how we were bound by the railroad tracks and streets that weren't paved with ditches running through them. The people who created segregation established and enforced these conditions to keep us away and to make us feel less than human. When I look back at it all, it is insulting to see how all of it played out. In Birmingham, there was a major interstate that was designed to divide an affluent Black neighborhood. There were many purposeful attempts to keep us divided.

Not too long ago, I attended an awards program at the Lyric Theater for a Civil Rights Institute event. They served us appetizers and wine. I was seated in the main section and had mixed feelings about being there. When I was growing up, I thought, The Lyric was the only integrated theater. Yes, it was integrated, except that we paid at the window and walked up a fire escape to view the movie from the balcony. We were paying the same price as White people but they walked in through the main door. I suppose we had to build a certain immunity to seeing and thinking about those things or else we would have been angry, and before civil rights, bad things happened to angry Blacks.

I wasn't bitter and some people can't understand why I didn't hate. I didn't know anyone to hate and didn't even know any Whites. Who was going to be the focus of my hate? Segregation had evolved and ran itself, so who was I going to blame? As you see, there are still a lot of unresolved feelings that are yet to be uncovered, but writing this story has helped me sort some of that out. As you have read in these last chapters, all of us who experienced the pain of separation and segregation dealt with the situation in a way that helped us survive and make sense of it. Now years later, we are still uncovering the pain that we buried deep within our hearts. Much like an onion, we will have to peel back each layer of pain and deal accordingly.

Speaking to audiences has been a part of my healing process. To see people's responses has helped to validate the experiences and my feelings about them. My journey with breast cancer allowed me time to think a lot about my past. It helped me understand the importance of continuing to tell my story loud and proud. Since having the chemo, I suffer from a post treatment impairment known as chemo-brain. Occasionally, I think of things in one way, but when I speak, my words come out a bit differently than I had formulated in my mind. That's why I needed to put this pen to this paper and tell my story while I still have time. God gave me a second chance and I have a legacy of love and justice to leave for my family. I'm marching on!

I am very proud to have been one of the hundreds who did stand up and say, "That's not fair," and who were willing to do what it took to turn the tide. I recognize that my going to jail was not as big a price to pay as those who were killed in the 16th Street Church bombing; that was the ultimate price to pay. I just don't want anyone to forget what it took to get us where we are today.

The Wesley family

ACKNOWLEDGEMENTS

I would like to express my gratitude to the many people who saw me through this book; to all those who provided support, talked things over, read, wrote, offered comments, allowed me to quote their remarks and assisted in the editing, proofreading and design. In particular, Dr. Martha Bouyer, a retired educator who currently serves as a member of the Jefferson County Board of Education (Birmingham, AL) was first to encourage me to write "my story." Her persistence finally led to the completion of this book.

Heartfelt gratitude is also extended to my friend, Kristy Rather, a Birmingham business professional who provided suggestions and assisted in the final editing. My appreciation is also extended to those who provided support in ascertaining documents and clarification of information. They include: Gregory Wilson, a history professor at Lawson State Community College, Bruce Wright, City Hall division of records; Paulette Porter Roby, Foot Soldiers Committee Chair; and Georgia Blair, member of the Birmingham Library Board.

Finally, I would like to thank my husband of forty-five years, Rufus D. Kelsey, for his support in this endeavor, allowing me the time away from home to share my story across the country and encouraging me to continue my fight for freedom.

To inquire about having Janice Kelsey speak at your school or civic group, contact her at:

kelseyjwk@aol.com